Collins

NORTH COAST 500
WHERE TO
EAT & STAY

Published by Collins
An imprint of HarperCollins Publishers
Westerhill Road
Bishopbriggs
Glasgow G64 2QT
www.harpercollins.co.uk

HarperCollins Publishers
Macken House,
39/40 Mayor Street Upper,
Dublin 1, D01 C9W8, Ireland

1st edition 2023

© HarperCollins Publishers 2023
Published in association with
North Coast 500 Ltd
Text written by Campbell Kerr
and Gemma Spence

NC500® and North Coast 500®
are registered trademarks of North
Coast 500 Ltd

Collins® is a registered trademark of
HarperCollins Publishers Ltd

The contents of this publication are
believed correct at the time of printing.
Nevertheless the publisher can accept
no responsibility for errors or omissions,
changes in the detail given or for any
expense or loss thereby caused.

HarperCollins does not warrant that
any website mentioned in this title will
be provided uninterrupted, that any
website will be error free, that defects
will be corrected, or that the website or
the server that makes it available are
free of viruses or bugs. For full terms
and conditions please refer to the site
terms provided on the website.

A catalogue record for this book is
available from the British Library

ISBN 978-0-00-854706-6

10 9 8 7 6 5 4 3

Printed in India

If you would like to comment on any
aspect of this book, please contact us
at the above address or online.
e-mail:
collins.reference@harpercollins.co.uk
 facebook.com/collinsref
 @collins_ref

Collins

NC5⊙⊙
• THE ULTIMATE ROAD TRIP •

NORTH COAST 500
WHERE TO
EAT & STAY

CONTENTS

£   A simple place that won't break the bank, probably somewhere to stop off for a coffee and quick snack.

££   Somewhere a little pricier, where you'd possibly have a meal and linger a while.

£££   A more luxurious spot, good for a special occasion or just to spoil yourself a little.

♿   Wheelchair accessible

🐕   Pet friendly

📶   WIFI available

🚗   EVC available

🌿   Vegetarian options available

🌾   Gluten free options available

NC5⦿O   NC500 member

/// what3words

Evie

Harray

Stennes

Kirkwall

Stromness

Hoy

Burray

Grimness

Cape Wrath

Balnakeil Craft Village

Durness

Talmine

Armadale

Strathy

Dunnet Head

Brough

Mey

John o' Groats

Scrabster

Forss

Castletown

Upper Gills

Coldbackie

Bettyhill

Borgie

Melvich

Thurso

Auckengill

Keiss

Kinlochbervie

Tongue

Halkirk

Noss Head

Inshegra

Wick

Puldagon

Scourie

Thrumster

Raffin

Drumbeg

Kylesku

Lybster

Clachtoll

Nedd

Unapool

Dunbeath

Latheron

Achmelvich

Baddidarroch

Inverkirkaig

Inchnadamph

Berriedale

Lochinver

Helmsdale

Achiltibuie

Lairg

Rosehall

Torroble

Brora

Ardmair

Morefield

In
Invershin

Golspie

Laide

Ullapool

Bonar Bridge

Evelix

Embo

Ormiscaig

Loggie

Ardgay

Dornoch

Poolewe

Dundonnell

Edderton

Tain

Portmahomack

Gairloch

Ardross

Fearn

achro

Talladale

Alness

Delny

Nigg

Balintore

Kinlochewe

Evanton

Invergordon

Garve

Dingwall

Cromarty

Torridon

Anchasheen

Strathpeffer

Fortrose

Rosemarkie

ieldaig

Annat

Munlochy

Avoch

Applecross

Muir of Ord

Kessock

Beauly

Inverness

rdarroch

Strathcarron

Lochcarron

Cannich

elvaig

INTRODUCTION

Known throughout the world as the land of myth and legend, the incredible highlands of Scotland have no shortage of ancient castles, secluded beaches, towering mountains, and crashing waterfalls. And the best part? All of the above can be found neatly married together along the very northern stretch of coastline forming the 516-mile road trip known as the North Coast 500 (NC500).

This world-famous road trip takes you on a journey through six ancient regions of the Scottish highlands: Inverness-shire, the Black Isle, Easter Ross, Sutherland, Caithness, and Wester Ross. The route tours along the stunning Scottish landscape and also takes travellers on a journey through history, providing a fascinating and enlightening trip through time.

Each area of the highlands has its own unique cultural and historical tales to share, dating from the lesser-known role the remote lands played in the Second World War, all the way back to the first footfalls of the Vikings on mainland Britain.

Starting in the highland capital of Inverness, the route can be enjoyed in either direction, but we have travelled in an anti-clockwise direction in this book, saving the dramatic landscape of Wester Ross for last. As the road winds through the remote highlands, the beauty of Scotland changes from a vast and open wilderness to an impenetrable wall of mountains and glens; a truly breathtaking sight to behold.

The first part of the trip takes you on a tour of the history and culture of the city of Inverness, before heading north into more remote lands. The red sandstone buildings of the city reflecting on the peaceful waters of the River Ness make it the perfect place to stretch the legs before the long journey north begins.

As the road turns north through the quaint harbour towns of the Black Isle and into the region of Easter Ross, the main route of the A9 cuts a direct route north across the Moray Firth, Cromarty Firth, and the Dornoch Firth. Don't be afraid to stray from the path, however, as you will find plenty of hidden gems lying westwards towards the quaint town of Beauly, or out towards the eastern coastline and the cute harbourside towns of Portmahomack and Shandwick.

Venturing into the largest of the northern regions, the ancient land of Sutherland, you may be curious as to why the second most northerly area of the British mainland is referred to in such a way. The origin of the name Sutherland is believed to date back to the time when Vikings arrived on the northern coast of Scotland. The Scandinavian invaders referred to the lands to the south of their home as the "Southern Land".

With a maximum altitude of just 706m, the landscape of Caithness is a stark contrast to the rest of the highlands of Scotland and has a fascinating story to tell as to why this is. The region of Caithness is actually home to a huge expanse of peatland known as a blanket bog. In fact, the so called "Flow Country" of Caithness is the largest blanket bog in Europe. A blanket bog is a unique habitat for wildlife which is created by large amounts of rainfall with very little evaporation; a key characteristic of the northern regions of the British Isles, as any local will gladly tell you.

Leaving the vast expanse of peatland behind, the road winds its way west along the northern coast of Scotland. Entering back into Sutherland, the path leads once more through the mountains and glens. Skirting the edges of tranquil sea lochs and winding in and out of the jagged and stunning coastline, the view on the right is of an endless ocean whilst the view to the left is that of weathered peaks and deep, alluring glens.

It is in this area of northern Scotland that the road narrows, filing down to a single track passage with passing places, and winding through the obstacles that Mother Nature created over millions of years. The road skips its way across the shallow bay of Tongue, with the impressive outline of Ben Loyal to the left and Castle Varrich sitting watchful high above the water, before winding its way along Loch Eriboll, a sea loch that cuts deep into the northern coastline of Scotland.

This marks the beginning of the descent down Scotland's western coast, arguably the most rugged and beautiful part of the UK. Keep an eye out for the famous Ceannabeinne Beach as you approach the town of Durness, a town famous for its historical links to the Viking age, as well as the stunning sandy beaches it has to behold, such as Balnakeil and Sango Sands.

Leaving behind this quaint town, the sight before you is one of unimaginable wilderness, as you approach the beginnings of Scotland's most remote region, Cape Wrath. The entire northwestern region of Scotland sits almost completely untouched, aside from a smattering of houses to the south of the peninsula, and one entirely remote, isolated, and quite perplexing cafe to the north peninsula at Cape Wrath Lighthouse, known as Ozone Cafe.

Heading south along the western shore, the difference in lifestyle that exists up in these remote parts of the world is obvious. It is a life more in touch with the beauty and serenity of the surroundings, and one that happens at a pace set by the shifting of the tide and the changing of the winds, rather than a schedule set out crudely by humankind. Embrace the opportunity to enjoy scenery that is so rare to find in this world and enjoy this final stint of your NC500 adventure at a slower pace.

Following the coast south as Sutherland turns into Wester Ross, the towns and villages that you pass through along the way all have their own stories to share and views to enjoy, from the crystal clear waters of Scourie Bay to the bustling sea port of Ullapool. With the boats offloading their daily catch, seafood does not get much fresher than this so make the most of it at the many award-winning restaurants in this beautiful part of the world.

With the small town of Applecross as your final resting place, soak up the welcoming atmosphere that the highlands enjoys so much, from the friendly locals to the fellow visitors all happily sharing tales from their own adventures. A cold drink, a friendly chat, and a stunning view. What better way is there to round of your road trip of a lifetime on the North Coast 500?

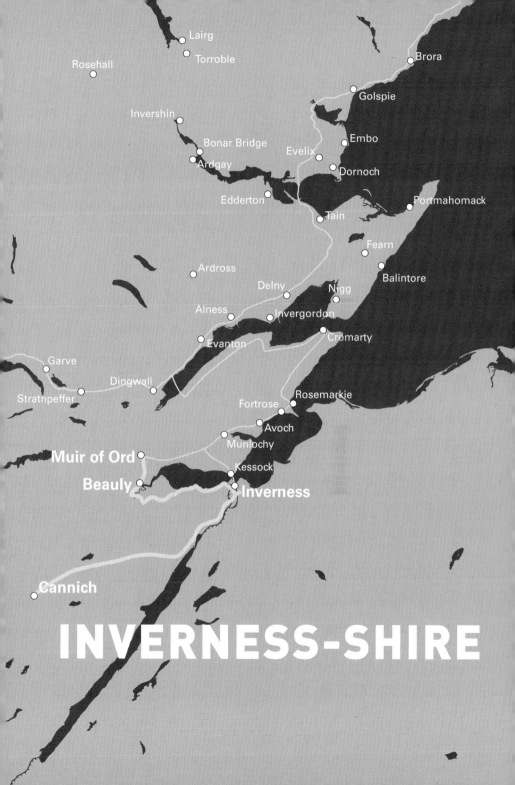

Cairngorms National Park

HIGHLAND RETREATS, Cannich

STAY
££
NC500

South of Inverness, around 15 miles to the west of the famous Loch Ness, sit the luxury lodges of the Highland Retreats in Cannich. These newly built, stylish, and very comfortable lodges are the perfect location for exploring the area to the south of Inverness, such as the nature reserve of Glen Affric, the nearby hidden gem of Dog Falls, or, of course, Scotland's most famous loch, Loch Ness.

The lodges themselves contain self-catering facilities with all of the cooking equipment you will need, as well as an external decking area to relax in the light summer evenings. Comfortable and welcoming, this accommodation is perfect for families wishing to explore the north of Scotland.
///flip.lump.polar

AMBIANCE CAFE, Inverness

EAT
£

Found inside the vibrant and atmospheric Victorian Market in the heart of Inverness, the Ambiance Cafe directly reflects its name as a welcoming and friendly spot for food and drink. If you are planning a day out exploring the city of Inverness then this is the perfect stop-off for a hearty breakfast, a great coffee, and some friendly recommendations from the local staff.
///influencing.precautions.empire

ARDTOWER CARAVAN PARK, Inverness

STAY
£££

This award-winning caravan park is situated perfectly between the bustling city of Inverness and the famous Culloden Battlefield, meaning there are plenty of activities and sights, as well as easy access to the bars, restaurants, and nightclubs of the city. As far as campsites go, the facilities on offer at Ardtower border on that of a luxury hotel, with a newly designed toilet and shower block featuring underfloor heating and accessible amenities.

This campsite also has an onsite playpark for children, a cafe and pizza restaurant for morning and evening meals, and boasts that 95% of the hard-standing pitches enjoy a stunning view of the Black Isle and beyond.
///inflame.brew.hoaxes

AUCHNAHILLIN HOLIDAY PARK, Inverness
The perfect stopover on your way north to the city of Inverness, Auchnahillin Holiday Park is situated just 10 minutes to the south of the capital of the highlands. This friendly, family-run holiday park is an ideal base for those wishing to tour the eastern region of Inverness, such as the beautiful Moray coastline, the famous Scotch Whisky Trail, or even the northern region of the UK's largest national park, the Cairngorms.

Onsite you will find 10 self-contained and fully equipped static caravans, as well as a number of touring pitches for tents, caravans and motorhomes.
///aquatics.washable.clutter

THE BAKERY, Inverness
Established in Inverness, The Bakery has since become one of the most popular places for freshly baked goods in Inverness. Located on the corner of Tomnahurich Street in Inverness, The Bakery serves delicious sourdough bread, freshly made sandwiches and pies to name a few, and also caters to vegetarians. Their pastries are top class and a popular purchase for breakfast, especially as they open at 6am.

There is a small car park around the corner from The Bakery in Montague Row with space for around four cars. There is limited seating at The Bakery, with only a couple of chairs and a table outside on the street, however it is the perfect place for a take-away breakfast or lunch to take down and enjoy by Ness River.
///woes.uses.tiles

A view of Ardross Terrace, Inverness

BEAUFORT COTTAGES, Inverness

A great base to start your North Coast 500 adventure from is the Beaufort Cottages. With a selection of properties from a pod, shepherd's hut and cottage, there are plenty of options for you to have a memorable start to your holiday.

Beaufort Cottages are located 12 miles outside the city of Inverness and only 2.5 miles from the delightful village of Beauly.

The village of Beauly is a great place to explore at the start of your trip, with many lovely cafes and restaurants in the area, as well as the Robertson's Farm Shop where you can get to see some beautiful highland cows.
///punters.sleeps.bedrock

THE BIKE SHED, Inverness

The Bike Shed is a small coffee house and events venue with a wooden rustic interior, located on Grant Street near the River Ness. As well as serving delicious, great value coffee and other hot drinks, The Bike Shed also hosts art exhibitions, craft workshops and live music to name a few. Head down on a Friday evening to enjoy the open mic night. There is parking available on the street outside The Bike Shed or around the corner on Simpson Lane.

The opening hours at the Bike Shed are limited, check out their Facebook page for up-to-date opening times before visiting.
///live.accent.parade

THE BLACK ISLE BAR AND ROOMS, INVERNESS

If you are looking for delicious wood-fired pizzas in the city centre, then you need to pay a visit to The Black Isle Bar. Originating in making world-class organic beer, The Black Isle Bar was founded in 1998 and now has two bars in Inverness and Fort William, as well as a boutique hostel on the Black Isle.

This cosy escape from the outdoors invites you in with delicious smells and a friendly atmosphere. Dietary requirements are considered and vegan and gluten-free options are available on the menu.

///looked.camera.parade

BLACK ISLE HOSTEL, Inverness

The Black Isle Hostel is conveniently located in the heart of Inverness, within walking distance from both the bus and the train station. The hostel hosts 10 mixed dorm rooms, sleeping four or six guests, as well as two private double rooms. Each bed features a USB charging point as well as a socket. A brilliant feature at the Black Isle Hostel is the room dedicated to drying your clothes after a wet day out in the highlands.

There is a lounge and dining area where guests can socialise and relax, making use of the travel books and maps to plan their next adventure. The kitchen area offers the use of two induction hobs, a toaster and a microwave.

There are storage facilities for those travelling on a bike or with extra luggage.

///ground.jazz.menu

BLEND TEA AND COFFEE MERCHANTS, Inverness

A local tea and coffee merchants in the heart of Inverness with over 20 different hand-blended loose teas on offer, and a whole lot more to it than just that. This small cafe is a favourite for breakfast and lunch for locals and tourists alike, with a large selection of locally sourced and freshly prepared meals.

The Black Isle Bar, Inverness

From fresh tea to bubble tea, pancakes and waffles to traditional Scottish breakfasts, this cafe has something for everyone, all served with a friendly and welcoming Highland smile. One of the top recommendations for Blend is the gourmet bagels on offer, particularly the "locally caught" vegetarian haggis!
///chins.tennis.shady

BUNCHREW CARAVAN PARK, Inverness

STAY
££

With incredible views of the tranquil waters of the Beauly Firth, Bunchrew Caravan Park is the perfect location for a relaxing getaway just five miles from Inverness. With 125 level pitches for tents, caravans and motorhomes, as well as 12 holiday caravans and two eco-cabins, this hugely popular campsite has everything you could need on your visit to Scotland.

There is even an onsite shop for all of the basic essentials, as well as a catering van during the peak summer season that provides breakfast and dinner, so you don't need to worry about cooking after a long day of exploration.
///digs.digesting.bother

CAFE ARTYSANS, Inverness

EAT
£

Just a short walk from Inverness train station sits the modern and relaxed Cafe Artysans, a fantastic option for freshly prepared and delicious food, all made in-house with a team that aims to make a difference.

Cafe Artysans is a social enterprise and is part of the Calman Trust Group, a charity that aims to develop the lives of young people by teaching life skills and helping them to take their next step into the world. Not only does your custom help to train and develop the skills and confidence of the local youngsters, every penny you spend is invested straight back in to the fantastic work that this charity does with the young people of the highlands.

Vegan breakfasts and lunch specials are also available.
///plans.skirt.good

CAFE DE PAULO, Inverness

A gem of a cafe in the heart of Inverness city centre, the Cafe de Paulo is a regular for locals and tourists alike for breakfasts and lunches. A great menu and good selection of vegetarian dishes are supported by a take-away service. The cafe also has a seating area beside the gift shop in the covered Victorian arcade/Market.
///broken.losses.pages

CAFE NESS BY THE CATHEDRAL, Inverness

Homemade cake and good coffee is the way to many peoples' hearts and at Cafe Ness by the Cathedral you will get just that, along with a warm welcome too. Located behind Inverness Cathedral, this social enterprise business also offers a range of hot foods, sandwiches and rolls, and a specials menu in line with the season. They cater for both vegetarian and vegan dietary requirements alongside meat and fish options on their menu.

A charitable 'suspended coffee programme' is carried out at Cafe Ness, enabling customers to purchase a hot drink and give to those in need.
///senses.video.treat

CAFE ONE, Inverness

Located on Castle Street, just off the High Street, Cafe One is a restaurant and wine bar with an expansive menu, serving delicious, unique dishes using fresh local ingredients. Cafe One is family run and you will be welcomed by a great team into a warm and friendly atmosphere. The restaurant can cater for brunch, lunch and dinner and has a range of vegetarian and vegan options on the menu. The Minions menu for children is excellent and very reasonably priced, while their Early Bird menu that offers some tasty dishes for a great price during the afternoon.
///salon.hiking.obey

The Victorian Market, Inverness

THE CALEDONIAN, Inverness

If you are looking for some good pub grub and a beer garden, The Caledonian is the place to go. Conveniently located on the High Street in Inverness, it is the perfect place to stop off for some food or drink after some shopping.

The food and drink at The Caledonian is very reasonably priced and the bar often has specials on throughout the day. ///orders.tilt.jumpy

CASTLE VIEW GUEST HOUSE, Inverness

Castle View is a comfortable, newly refurbished accommodation located in the heart of Inverness with incredible views of Inverness Castle across River Ness. There are a number of rooms at Castle View suitable for families as well as twin, double king and super king rooms, all of which come with en-suite bathrooms and a TV.

Enjoy a traditional Scottish home-cooked breakfast or buffet style continental breakfast looking across to Inverness Castle. Vegetarian and vegan options are available. ///police.glass.mock

CHEESE AND TOMATIN, Inverness

Sitting above the bustling high street of Inverness town centre is the hugely popular authentic Italian pizza joint, Cheese and Tomatin. Its name gently playing on the nearby location of Tomatin, this cosy restaurant focuses on gourmet wood-fired pizzas, hand-crafted with experience and passion. No matter what your preferred toppings may be – from a simple mozzarella to a spicy nduja – Cheese and Tomatin has just the pizza for you. And that's not to forget their speciality dessert pizzas, such as Nutella with cooked bananas.

The intimate setting of the adjoining 18th Century cottages means that seating is limited to just 27 people, 20 in the main seating area at No.12 and room for a party of up to seven people in

the cosy upstairs room at No.10. Therefore, booking in advance is always recommended to ensure you don't go hungry. This small, family run business also provides take-away and delivery services if you would rather eat in the comfort of your home or fancy a pizza with a view from the top of castle hill.
///kept.solo.wipe

COFFEE AFFAIR, Inverness

EAT
£

Coffee Affair is a spacious coffee shop in the city centre of Inverness. It serves up breakfast and lunch options with vegetarian and vegan options. When you walk in, your eyes will be met with a delicious display of pastries and cakes.

It is worth noting, however, that there is no laptop use allowed in this social hub, so if you are in need of a digital fix then this isn't the spot for you.
///search.tribe.spots

COLUMBA HOTEL, Inverness

EAT &
STAY
££

The 3-star Columba Hotel is perfectly located in the city centre, boasting spectacular views of the tranquil waters of River Ness and the impressive silhouette of Inverness Castle. The grand exterior of this hotel is matched with the beautiful contemporary decor of its interior, with bright and spacious guest rooms offering the latest modern facilities, such as TV and high-speed internet.

In addition to the grand interior, central location, stunning views, and complimentary breakfast, the most common highlight for visitors spending the night at the Columba is the friendliness and hospitality of the hard-working staff, welcoming you at the door and doing everything they can to ensure you have the best stay possible.
///hogs.lonely.last

Columba Hotel, Inverness

THE COO'S GUEST HOUSE, Inverness

STAY
££

The Coo's Guest House is a conveniently located family run hotel that dates back to the beginning of Twentieth century. There are nine bedrooms that are newly refurbished and are very spacious with a smart TV. The friendly hosts welcome you with open arms to heart of Inverness and offer you a complimentary breakfast each morning during your stay.

The Coo's Guest House is within walking distance of many 4great attractions in the city centre of Inverness.
///lift.cats.poppy

COYOTE BURGER, Inverness

EAT
£££

Offering take-away and eat-in options, Coyote Burger is a superb place to dine in Inverness. Located along the river on Bank Street, this restaurant is perfectly located in the city centre making it a very popular place to go for a premium burger.

The menu at Coyote Burger will have your stomach rumbling, with a great selection of beef, chicken, vegetarian and vegan choices with the option to add on a side of their popular 'dirty fries'. The Coyote Secret Burger Sauce pot is a very popular topping that you may consider trying on your burger of choice. If you want to make a meal of Coyote Burger, try their Coyote Combo Meals for a bit of a discount.
///teeth.kinks.smooth

CULLODEN MOOR CARAVAN PARK, Inverness

EAT
£

Situated near the site of one of Scotland's most significant battles, one that completely rewrote the history of the nation, Culloden Moor Caravan and Motorhome Club site is a beautiful place to stay on the outskirts of the city of Inverness. The location is a beautifully secluded spot for a relaxing holiday in the lower highlands of Scotland, with stunning views of the Nairn Valley and easy access to the city centre of the highland capital.

It was here, just six miles from Inverness city centre, that Bonnie Prince Charlie was defeated at Culloden Battlefield, a battle

that changed the course of the Jacobite Rebellion and the history of Scotland forever. As well as this nearby historical site, the Culloden Moor Caravan Park offers easy access to the Moray region to the east, the Speyside Whisky Trail and the enchanting region of Glen Affric.
///verbs.luggage.gobblers

EAT
£

CUP & CONE, Inverness

Super friendly service, great coffee, and delicious toasted sandwiches, this cute and cosy cafe sitting just to the east of Inverness city centre is a huge hit with locals and tourists alike. The minimalist decor of this cafe matches nicely with the simple and stress-free menu it has to offer.

Entering into Cup & Cone, have a quick glance at the hot drink and ice-cream menus on the wall before taking your time to peruse the range of freshly made cakes that sit proudly on display inside the counter. No matter what has brought you to the cafe for the day, be it a sweet treat or a simple coffee, the window-facing bench is always a perfect spot to watch the world go by and let your thoughts run away from you.
///laser.span.shed

EAT
££

ENCORE, Inverness

A stone's throw from Ness Bridge and Inverness Castle, Encore Une Fois is a celebration of the local history of Inverness, the food that it has to offer, and the highland way of life. Inspired by the mission of the Jacobite Uprising and Bonnie Prince Charlie, Encore serves up a selection of highland favourites, from morning through to evening.

Join the celebration of the highland way of life with live music throughout the week, featuring local musicians and karaoke nights, all in a warm and welcoming atmosphere. It is also the perfect place to sample some of Scotland's famous whisky, with a selection of over 50 drams to choose from. Make the most of your time in Inverness the highland way and spend an evening in good company at this local bar and restaurant.
///hoping.lovely.shops

Leanach Cottage at Culloden Battlefield

EAT
£

STAY
£££

NC500

EAT
£

FIG AND THISTLE, Inverness

Located in the heart of Inverness city centre, the Fig and Thistle offers a warm welcome into its Bistro where delicious, modern Scottish cuisine is served in a relaxed and friendly environment. This highly rated cafe/bistro is noted as one of the best in Inverness and sources its produce sustainably from around the country, bringing it together in a delicious celebration of local cuisine. A must visit.

///animal.metro.stove

FRISCO VILLAS, Inverness

Book yourself a luxurious stay in the Highlands at Frisco Villas, a luxury accommodation in Inverness. This boutique hotel features amenities that take this property to the next level, such as a large copper bathtub and a powerful double-width rainfall shower. The interior of this Victorian villa apartment is outstanding and makes for a very relaxing stay within walking distance of the city centre.

Frisco Villas is a great base for exploring the start of the NC500 route, whether you choose to see the sights around the city centre or venture further afield to visit locations such as Loch Ness or Culloden Battlefield.

///outer.town.needed

THE GELLIONS, Inverness

A classic Scottish bar with a cracking atmosphere in the heart of Inverness. Situated on Bridge Street, The Gellions is the oldest pub in Inverness. This bar and live music venue has been around since 1841 and there is live music playing here seven nights a week. You will always find at least eight Scottish beers on tap at The Gellions as well as an extensive range of Scottish gins and whiskies.

///market.turns.volunteered

GLEN MHOR HOTEL, Inverness

The Glen Mhor Hotel sits in the heart of the city centre of Inverness and offers a unique stay across its selection of rooms. 10 attractive Victorian buildings host 110 bedrooms between them. These are set across 11 self-contained apartments and a luxury villa with four bedrooms, the River Ness Villa.
///nails.pill.lately

EAT &
STAY
££

GRAIN AND GRIND, Inverness

Grain and Grind is popular, bright and spacious coffee-shop in the heart of Inverness which serves the most delicious hot drinks, cakes and hot food. The vibe inside is calm as you are met by the friendly staff.

EAT
££

Grain and Grind started off as a coffee shop and has now grown into a roastery and seven coffee shops, six of these being in Glasgow. They supply other small shops and coffee shops around the highlands with their coffee beans and also their compostable coffee bags, which are biodegradable. If you enjoy your drink in their cafe then make sure to stock up on a bag for yourself to take home.

As well as serving their speciality coffee, they also offer a specialty list of hot chocolates that are decadent in flavour. Even their 'normal' hot chocolate is made using ganache, which gives it a delicious creamy texture in combination with the deep chocolate flavour. Plant-based milk is also offered.

Grain and Grind caters to your dietary requirements with many vegetarian, vegan and gluten-free options in both the hot food and cake selection.
///audit.loaf.sweat

Heathmount Hotel, Inverness

THE HEATHMOUNT HOTEL BAR AND KITCHEN, Inverness

The Heathmount Hotel is a small family owned hotel on the outskirts of the city centre of Inverness. This boutique hotel has a modern interior and features a stylish bar and restaurant serving locally sourced food and drinks from independent breweries.

The hotel is dog-friendly and the luxury bedrooms feature power showers in the en-suite.
///couple.train.long

HIGHLAND ESCAPE, Inverness

Located in one of the most beautiful places in the world, the Highland Escape offers you a special trip to Loch Ness with beautiful unspoilt views overlooking the Loch, where Nessie has apparently once been spotted. This accommodation features six large guest rooms, rented out as a whole, and you can choose whether you wish for a self-catered or fully catered stay.

The charming Scottish interiors, along with the fireplace and cosy snug room make for a very comfortable and stylish stay in this stunning location. There is an immense amount of history, including captivating castles of myth and legend, in the area which is the perfect way to begin your North Coast 500 adventure.
///acrobatic.outermost.unfair

INVERNESS YOUTH HOSTEL, Inverness

Just a short walk from the city centre of Inverness, the budget accommodation of the Inverness Youth Hostel is a popular choice for solo travellers, families, and groups of adventurers looking for somewhere affordable and reliable. As it is a 4-star accredited Visit Scotland hostel accommodation, you can rest assured that any stay here will be a comfortable and reliable place to rest your head.

With an onsite cafe and a well-equipped self-catering facility, this hostel offers the choice of either cooking for yourself or relaxing and dining out for breakfast, lunch, or dinner.
///gravel.hope.overnight

EAT & STAY ££

NC500

STAY £££

NC500

STAY £

NC500

KINGSMILL HOTEL, Inverness

The Kingsmill Hotel is a large 4-star hotel located very close to the city centre of Inverness, yet feels like you are in the middle of nature. This 4-star hotel has 147 rooms with family rooms, bunk spaces and dog-friendly rooms. They also have 13 garden rooms, tailoring guest experiences and giving you the feeling of being out in the countryside.

The hotel features a leisure club with a swimming pool, sauna, steam room, jacuzzi and a gym, as well as a spa and beauty hair salon on site. The toiletries used are local to Scotland, refreshing your skin and leaving your hands smelling delightful.

The Inglis Restaurant welcomes you to taste some of the exciting flavours of Scottish food on the menu created by its Belgian chef. From seafood to vegan meals there is something for everyone on the menu here. There is also the option to enjoy an afternoon tea in the lounge area or to try some of the extensive whisky range in the whisky bar.
///proud.asset.plan

THE KITCHEN BRASSERIE, Inverness

One of the most loved restaurants in Inverness is The Kitchen Brasserie. With beautiful views from three floors overlooking Inverness Castle and Ness River, this restaurant also offers a heated terrace area which is sublime during the warmer and drier months. The service at The Kitchen Brasserie is unforgettable and the flavours executed through the food are exquisite. Perfect for a special occasion or just to treat yourself.
///camp.trying.audio

LITTLE ITALY, Inverness

This restaurant is the only traditional Italian-owned restaurant in Inverness and it is loved by many as a little slice of Italy in the Highland city. There is a cosy atmosphere indoors where you can enjoy a selection of wines alongside delicious Italian dishes. Little Italy is willing to cater to dietary requirements. If the weather is nice, there is an outdoor seating area overlooking the High Street of Inverness.
///hulk.jazz.issue

Kingsmill Hotel, Inverness

EAT
££

MACGREGORS, Inverness

MacGregors Bar and Restaurant is a welcoming and friendly venue in the centre of Inverness. The menu hosts a selection of vegetarian and vegan options, however one of their most popular events is the Sunday roast. We recommend visiting this top traditional Scottish bar on a late Sunday afternoon to enjoy the live music open session, where musicians come together and play traditional Scottish music. You will feel a part of the family after visiting this bar and, depending when you visit, there may even be an intimate live event downstairs.

The large bi folding doors open up into a spacious beer garden which is perfect for enjoying a cold beverage during the summer months.
///head.hope.gasp

DRINK
££

NC500

MALT ROOM, Inverness

The best way to get into the highland frame of mind, the Malt Room is Inverness' first dedicated whisky bar. Offering a range of tasting menus, individual drams, and even speciality cocktails, wines and beers, this small and intimate bar is the best way to sample the best that Scotland has to offer.

Begin your NC500 adventure with a tasting flight of the best whiskies that you will find around the 516-mile route and have a chat with the experienced bartenders about the stories each taste, smell, and bottle has to tell. With over 200 different malts, you are sure to find the whisky note that is perfect for you.
///drag.weedy.nods

DRINK
££

MARKET BAR, Inverness

Tucked away from the bustling High Street of Inverness is the small, cute, and lively music venue known as the Market Bar. Regarded as more "music with a bar, than a bar with music", the intimate and unique setting of this bar is one that is highly recommended to anyone wishing to experience the most authentic side to Inverness.

Although Market Bar does not serve up food, the daily performances of local live musicians is sure to make your visit to Inverness one to remember. At one point in time, Market Bar showcased early performances of big names such as The Proclaimers, Paolo Nutini, Billy Connolly, and Amy Mcdonald, so keep in mind that your visit to Market Bar may just go down in the history of Scotland's future talent.

On a more supernatural side, as one of the oldest bars in Inverness, dating back to 1740, regular visitors to Market Bar tell tales of footsteps being heard and fingerprints appearing around the bar with no apparent host to explain them. Don't worry about these tales, however, as the owners of the bar insist that any presence felt by patrons has always felt friendly and welcoming.

It seems even ghosts will greet you with a warm highland welcome up this way.
///stared.verge.trains

MCBAIN'S BY THE RIVER, Inverness

McBain's By The River is a small, family-run restaurant on the River Ness in Inverness. The family has over 22 years experience in the hospitality field which is reflected in their service and meals. McBain's By The River is open for lunch and dinner and offers an A la Carte and a Pre-theatre menu deal with a delicious selection of dishes.

Staff can cater for allergy or dietary requirements and all ingredients are fresh and locally sourced and served to you either in the restaurant or at the outdoor seating area overlooking the river.
///swear.hoot.breed

MacGregors, Inverness

MILK BAR, Inverness

Serving up locally roasted and freshly prepared coffee from the Inverness Roasting Company, the Milk Bar is a fantastic stop-off for your daily caffeine fix. Rated as one of Inverness's top spots for desserts, it's known for its delicious ice-cream, baked goods, and milkshakes, as well as its wide range of plant-based alternatives.

This small cafe has seating available in the bustling market hall of the historical Victorian Market in Inverness city centre, making it perfect for enjoying the vibrant atmosphere of the city while enjoying some of the best treats that the highlands has to offer.
///cubs.safe.driver

THE MUSTARD SEED, Inverness

Situated in an old converted church building with an outdoor balcony seating area overlooking the river, The Mustard Seed is one of the most popular restaurants in Inverness. If the weather isn't on your side, cosy up indoors in front of the wood-burning fire.

This unique space has kept many of the original features of the church building intertwined with modern character creating a lovely atmosphere. The menu has a wide range of classy dishes ranging from meat, seafood and vegan options.
///activism.issued.outfit

NESS LODGES, Inverness

Zoe and Billy are the proud owners of Ness Lodge and Wee Ness Lodge, two beautiful accommodations in the city centre of Inverness. Overlooking the Ness River you don't feel like you are only a 10-minute walk away from the High Street. Zoe and Billy have travelled a lot themselves and know exactly what is needed to create a home away from home. Every last detail has been considered and a special touch includes the food and drink that is in the fridge on your arrival.

NC500

Wee Ness Lodge was inspired by a trip to Norway. It is built with Western Red Cedar and, combined with floor-length glass windows overlooking the river, gives a feeling of complete remoteness.
///empire.policy.tigers

NESS WALK, Inverness
Ness Walk is a luxury accommodation in the heart of Inverness, offering a 5-star service to its guests. The original 19th century building is listed and was derelict before Ness Walk was born. The hotel has now been expanded around the original listed building to house 47 beautiful rooms and two suites.

On arrival, guests are offered a glass of complimentary champagne and are then shown to their room by the friendly staff. The team at Ness Walk are very passionate and nothing is too much for them.
///light.shirts.broom

NUMBER 27 BAR AND KITCHEN, Inverness
Number 27 Bar and Kitchen serves delicious locally, sourced food on Castle Street in Inverness. Vegetarian and vegan meals are offered on the menu and all of the meals are professionally presented.

The restaurant is open plan with a modern interior and comfortable atmosphere. An extensive wine list is available and the friendly trained staff are happy to offer recommendations. Other drinks served include a selection of gins, whiskies, lagers and even prosecco cocktails.
///salon.chins.causes

PERK COFFEE AND DONUTS, Inverness
Looking for a quirky and delicious cafe to "perk" up your afternoon exploring the city centre of Inverness? Then the small, friendly, and dangerously mouth-watering Perk Coffee and Doughnuts cafe is perfect for you. Pay a visit to this cute and

Ness Walk, Inverness

colourful doughnut shop on Church Street for their wide selection of handmade and incredibly decadent doughnuts that are sure to leave a lasting impression.

Due to the huge popularity of this locally owned cafe, the freshly prepared and hand-crafted doughnuts are known to start selling out from 1pm each day. However, not to worry if you can't make it before then as pre-orders for collection before 3pm are available, as well as delivery options for the local area.
///pink.police.gently

PRIME STEAK AND SEAFOOD, Inverness

If you are looking for a fresh catch in the city centre of Inverness, Prime Steak and Seafood is your go to. Specialising in lobster, and sticky toffee pudding, this restaurant serves a great selection of steak and fresh seafood alongside many other options. The staff at Prime Steak and Seafood pride themselves in sustainability, therefore all produce is sourced locally and vegetarian and vegan option are available, the bbq mushrooms being the most popular vegan option.
///pizza.notice.vocab

RENDEZVOUS VINTAGE CINEMA CAFE, Inverness

Visit Rendezvous Vintage Cinema Cafe if you are looking for the most recommended breakfast in Inverness. Serving up a selection of vegan, vegetarian and gluten-free options, this High Street cafe is a unique place to visit in the city centre. There is both indoor and outdoor seating or you can take away. The Beatles once played in this building, which was formerly a dance club, before becoming one of Inverness' most familiar cafes.
///grace.ports.hired

RIVER HOUSE RESTAURANT, Inverness

Overlooking the River Ness with views up to Inverness Castle, River House Restaurant offers the finest fresh seafood, sourced locally. Mussels, oysters and crab are a few of the options that are featured on the menu. Appetisers and sharing plates are also on offer to enjoy in this relaxed, plush environment.

The chef proprietor at the River House Restaurant, Alfie grew up in a small Cornish port and it was here that his strong admiration for the sea came from. Alfie also found his love for good food in Cornwall, where he was first introduced to fresh local produce and seafood.
///needed.broken.swung

EAT
£££

ROCPOOL, Inverness

A Michelin guide restaurant in the heart of Inverness with large glass windows displaying views of Inverness Castle across the river. The Rocpool is a family owned, independent, contemporary brasserie serving luxury dishes in a trendy interior.

Since first opening its doors in 2002, the Rocpool has grown a loyal fanbase in Inverness with many locals and tourists enjoying the unique menu, which offers a range of dishes including a selection of seafood, meat and vegetarian meals.
///levels.brass.cuts

EAT
£££

ROCPOOL RESERVE, Inverness

Situated just a stone's throw from the bustling city centre of the highland capital, the Rocpool Reserve offers a luxurious 5-star retreat for visitors on the first or last legs of their NC500 adventure. Offering the perfect combination of grandeur and minimalism, this boutique hotel, bar, and restaurant is sure to provide you with a comfortable stay that you will not forget anytime soon.

From the tastefully crafted menus to the comfort-centred rooms, with spa-style bathrooms and rainfall showers, every part of the Rocpool Reserve is designed to indulge guests in a luxury unique to the highlands of Scotland.
///gifted.fool.bugs

EAT &
STAY
£

NC500

Inverness Castle, Inverness

THE ROYAL HIGHLAND HOTEL, Inverness

EAT &
STAY
£££

The friendly staff at the Royal Highland Hotel will welcome you to your stay in Inverness. Located in the city centre, beside the train station, this convenient hotel has an interesting and unique Great Gatsby vibe, transporting you back to the 1900s. This hotel is only a five minute walk from many delicious city centre restaurants, or you can choose to enjoy a meal in the Ash Restaurant in the hotel.

The Royal Highland Hotel is the oldest hotel in Inverness, dating back to 1856 and has hosted guests such as the British Royal Family. It was restored in 2000 keeping its unique character and charm. The grand entrance and bifurcated staircase leads you towards 84 spacious rooms with high ceilings, passing some quirky paintings on the way.
///area.cult.doors

SAFFRON INDIAN, Inverness

EAT
££

Saffron Indian is a family run small restaurant and take-away cooking the most delicious traditional Indian cuisine. Located in Inverness, this restaurant offers dine-in, delivery and take-away food made using the freshest ingredients and locally sourced produce. Alcohol is not served at Saffron Indian, however you can bring your own beer or wine to enjoy with your meal.

The mission at Saffron Indian is to advance the experience of eating Indian cuisine whilst continuing to be affordable and accessible. It is also to important to the staff that you have an enjoyable dining experience, you can enjoy delicious food whilst also enjoying a welcoming and friendly service. It is recommended that you book a table in advance.
///pesky.convinces.enacted

SCOTCH AND RYE, Inverness

EAT
£

Scotch and Rye is a stylish cocktail bar and kitchen in the city centre of Inverness. Think 1920s America vibes and be transported back in time through their rustic industrial interior. The friendly bar staff are welcoming and open to suggesting recommendations based on your taste. The menu has a great selection and the dishes are full of flavour, offering a variety of options for differing dietary requirements.

There is a great atmosphere in the Scotch and Rye, which runs under the same company as The White House. Kick back in the bar and enjoy one of their two pint steins or vintage cocktails in this welcoming bar.
///best.formal.angel

THAI DINING, Inverness
Thai Dining is a gem of a restaurant in the Scottish Highlands offering delicious Thai cuisine in a friendly and welcoming atmosphere. This family run business has authenticity at the heart of the restaurant and staff have been serving up the most delicious traditional Thai food for almost a decade.

Transport yourself to the wonders of Southeast Asia with a visit to this Thai restaurant as you enjoy the Teak decor that was sourced directly from Thailand itself. With a dedicated vegan menu, this restaurant is also very welcoming to those with specific dietary requirements and is happy to make any adjustments necessary for you to enjoy your meal.

Thai Dining also offers take-away options for those wishing to enjoy the flavours of Asia in the comfort of their accommodation for the night, or perhaps in some of the beautiful Scottish summer sun.
///teeth.club.month

URQUHART'S, Inverness
Urquhart's Restaurant is a small, family run business consisting of Brian Urquhart as the chef and his daughter, Rachel working front of house. Urquhart's is a short walk away from the city centre of Inverness and serves a great selection of delicious home-cooked meals. On the menu you will find a variety of meat, fish and vegetarian dishes and if you have any specific dietary requirements, the staff are more than happy to help.
///ties.nights.shut

The Royal Highland Hotel, Inverness

THE VELOCITY BIKE SHOP, Inverness

Situated at the top of Steven's Street lies one of Inverness quirkier and more unique coffee stops, the Velocity Bike Shop. As soon as you enter into the cafe, meet the welcoming smiles from the staff and fellow customers and spot the bicycle hanging from the ceiling of the cafe, you know this place is one of a kind. This off-the-wall cafe offers everything from a creative and delicious food menu to backshop bike repairs and upgrades to everyone and anyone.

Hugely popular with the locals, this vegetarian and vegan cafe combines its incredible food with a forward-thinking zero waste policy, encouraging customers to bring take-away cups and tubs of their own for a discount on their meal/drink.
///honest.candle.legs

THE WATERFRONT, Inverness

The Waterfront opened over 100 years ago and was previously named 'Friars Shott'. Jamie, the General Manager and his team will always make sure your needs are catered for at The Waterfront and follow the motto "We have no strangers enter here … Only friends we have yet to meet".

Located on the banks of the River Ness, this bar and restaurant serves home-cooked food and a traditional Sunday lunch. The Head Chef Ros, alongside her team are passionate about creating great food using local produce and also cater to dietary requirements offering a selection of tasty vegetarian and vegan options that are also expertly prepared.

The Waterfront is located a five-minute walk from the city centre of Inverness, nestled between the bridges crossing over the river. There is paid parking available outside on the one way street.
///gifted.tens.toned

WATERSIDE RESTAURANT AT GLEN MHOR HOTEL, Inverness

EAT
STAY
£££

As the tranquil waters of River Ness flow by and the birds dance through the blooming trees above, a relaxing visit to the open beer garden of the Waterside Restaurant is the perfect way to spend a summer night in Inverness. This family friendly restaurant offers a range of menus from lunchtime to dinner, with a wide variety of food choices, including a kids menu and a vegan and vegetarian menu.
///nails.pill.lately

WHISK AWAY, Inverness

EAT
££

A cosy and quirky cafe serving up a range of breakfast and lunch items, all from locally sourced bakers, butchers, and coffee roasters, Whisk Away is a highly rated eatery with friendly staff and a great atmosphere.

Local business sits right at the heart of the Whisk Away mentality, as it proudly serves up breads from the local Three Little Bakers, meat from the local Hastie and Dyce butchers, and coffee from the Skye Coffee Roasters. Inside the cafe there is also a gift shop where you can browse the skilled craftwork from over 40 local artisans, in the form of pickles, jams, and chutneys, as well as handmade jewellery and candles.
///phones.wants.showed

THE WHITE HOUSE KITCHEN AND BAR, Inverness

EAT
£££

The White House Kitchen and Bar is a stylish cocktail bar and bistro in the centre of Inverness. The interior is elegant and comfortable, large windows making the area lovely and bright. Enjoy one of their delicious cocktails alongside a tasty dish from their menu, which caters to all dietary requirements.
///tender.cook.easy

The Velocity Bike Shop, Inverness

WILD WEE PANCAKES, Inverness

EAT
££

Everything from the decor to the food is organic and natural in Wild Pancakes. This cosy cafe offers a great selection of breakfast and lunch dishes, their speciality being the delicious pancakes that come with some incredible sweet or savoury toppings. There are vegan, dairy free and gluten-free options on the menu available for sitting in or taking away.

Well-behaved dogs are also welcome to come in and join the friendly atmosphere of this cafe in the heart of Inverness.
///slimy.wiped.hunt

XOKO BAKEHOUSE AND COFFEE BAR, Inverness

EAT
£

Fernando and Tristan welcome you into their open-plan bake house where love and passion is evidently poured into their baking. Pronounced "shaw-co" Xoko comes from the ancient Nahuatl language in Mexico. It means "The village where the bitter fruit grows", which is thought to be the origin of the word chocolate. This bakehouse and coffee bar is all about chocolate as Belgian chocolate is used in all of their products. Who wouldn't want to taste that?

Fernando is from Mexico and has worked across Latin America and Spain where he developed his passion for pastries and baking. Travel has inspired Fernando and Tristan's baking as their goods feature a flavour reminding you of travels outwith Scotland.

Located in the city centre of Inverness, you can sit outside and watch the world go by, or enjoy the atmosphere from the cosy bakehouse inside, smelling your cinnamon roll as it cooks in the oven.
///factor.lined.sleeps

BEAULY HOLIDAY PARK, Beauly

Beauly Holiday Park is a family run large touring site on the outskirts of the beautiful highland village of Beauly. This large campsite is open to both RVs and tents, as well as offering a passing service to those who require water and a chemical disposal point.

Alan and Lori will make your stay at Beauly Holiday Park very welcome; they have thought about everything the site needs in great detail, having travelled a lot themselves. The holiday park sits on the banks of the River Beauly and there are accessible points down to the river from the campsite. The nature walk at the end of the site is the perfect place to walk your dog and look out for the wildlife that roams in the area.
///shirtless.enforced.buyers

CAFE BIAGIOTTI, Beauly

Opened in 2017, the small and cute Cafe Biagiotti is owned by a local Italian family that is hugely popular with the locals for its freshly made cakes, pastries, filled focaccias, and many other delicious Italian delicacies. Named after the founder's grandmother, Cafe Biagiotti has a simple and cosy feel to it, with the lively chatter of the visitors echoing around the cafe and the smell of the handmade pizzettes wafting through the air.

If you are visiting the area and wish to take the taste of an authentic Italian meal home with you, Cafe Biagiotti has a Biagiotti at Home range, with its "Pasta at Home" experience. This allows you to enjoy freshly made pasta with a variety of sauces as well as instructions on how to prepare the dish in the comfort of your accommodation for the night, perhaps with a glass of wine or even a local whisky.
///badly.gardens.calibrate

CORNER ON THE SQUARE, Beauly

Marked by the vibrant chatter from the outdoor seating area, the unique deli-cafe, Corner on the Square, is a hotspot for locals and visitors alike. Highly rated for its freshly prepared food from the kitchen, as well as its coffee, cakes, and fresh produce on offer in its deli shop.

This locally owned delicatessen and eatery began in 2003 when the owner of the local fruit shop, Gary Williamson, decided to convert it from a doctor's surgery back to the deli store that it once was. This then evolved into a cafe as well, as Gary's wife Jacqui transformed the corner shop into a well-known and loved location for warm food and great customer service.

The Corner on the Square offers a wide range of fresh fruit and veg, baked goods, eggs & dairy goods, meats, seafood & poultry, as well as plenty of other locally sourced essentials that you may need on your NC500 adventure. Winner of multiple awards, such as the Independent Food & Drink retailer of the year in 2017 and 2019, you can't go wrong with a visit to the Corner on the Square deli-cafe.
///popping.factoring.romantics

THE FRIARY FISH AND CHIPS, Beauly

EAT
£

One of the specialities of the highlands of Scotland that is famous throughout the world is its locally sourced and fresh seafood. The Friary Fish and Chips takes full advantage this, serving up freshly caught and sustainably-sourced seafood, as well as the best quality potatoes for their chips.

End the day with a high and grab a good old fish and chips before you wave goodbye to the small village of Beauly. Our favourite way to end any day out in the highlands is with some hot chips and a seaside view, and in this part of Scotland you are simply spoiled for choice with both of these.
///onions.plantings.devoured

HARRY GOW, Beauly

EAT
££

Harry Gow is a bakery and take-away that is located around the east of the Scottish Highlands, with a total of 34 stores offering freshly baked goods. With over five generations of the family being involved in the company since 1979, this is far from a generic chain bakery, as all of their produce is made right here in the highlands of Scotland.

Voted Scottish Baker of the Year in 2019, Harry Gow is famous on the NC500 as a must-visit location for all tourists, especially with their ever expanding menu now catering for vegetarian and vegan diets. We highly recommend trying their delicious Dream Ring, as well as their vegan pies.
///slamming.branch.crackling

EAT & STAY ££

LOVAT ARMS HOTEL, Beauly
A simple stone's throw from the tranquil waters of the River Beauly you will find the grand hotel known as the Lovat Arms, situated right in the heart of the Scottish Highlands. Built in 1871, this hotel has been welcoming visitors to the highlands for over three decades and has been a main feature of the beautiful village of Beauly for over a century.

Located at the mouth of the Beauly Firth, the village of Beauly is often missed by visitors to the area, whom rather than taking the scenic route around the firth shoot straight up the A9, missing this peaceful and quaint town. Don't make this mistake on your visit to the highlands, however, as this small town is a gem that cannot be missed. So much so that it is believed that the name itself descends from the French words "Beau Lieu", or "beautiful place", coined by Mary Queen of Scots in 1230 when she stayed at the local priory.
///decimals.unscrew.sculpting

EAT & STAY £

NC500

ROOMS AT THE DOWNRIGHT GABBLER, Beauly
Overlooking Station Road in the cute village of Beauly sit the selection self-catering accommodation of the Apartments at the Gabbler and the Apartments at the Station. These newly developed, luxury spaces all contain their own mini kitchen, bedroom, and shower room.

In addition to the comfort and welcome that residents can expect from the Gabbler, a visit to these apartments also offers a culinary adventure of the history of the surrounding area. Offering dining experiences such as Living the Dram (a tale of the history of whisky), A Month of Sundays (the story of the traditional Sunday lunch), and Ale & Hearty (the tale of the role that beer has played in Scottish history), a meal at the Gabbler is unlike any you will experience anywhere else.

///tabloid.rifled.trapdoor

SHIMLA INDIAN RESTAURANT AND TAKE-AWAY, Beauly

EAT
££

Serving up quality Indian and Bangladeshi cuisine in the heart of the highland village of Beauly is the Shimla Indian restaurant. Open seven days a week, this is the perfect location for any visitors looking for a delicious and freshly prepared meal served up in a warm and welcoming environment. Or for those who would rather enjoy a curry in the comfort of their own homes, Shimla also offers a delivery service to the local area.

The menu is wide and varied, offering a host of authentic Indian and Bangladeshi curries, all of which are crafted with passion and experience. There is a good choice of vegetarian options and for those with specific dietary requirements, the staff are happy to adapt any recipe as suitable.

///javelin.necklace.merely

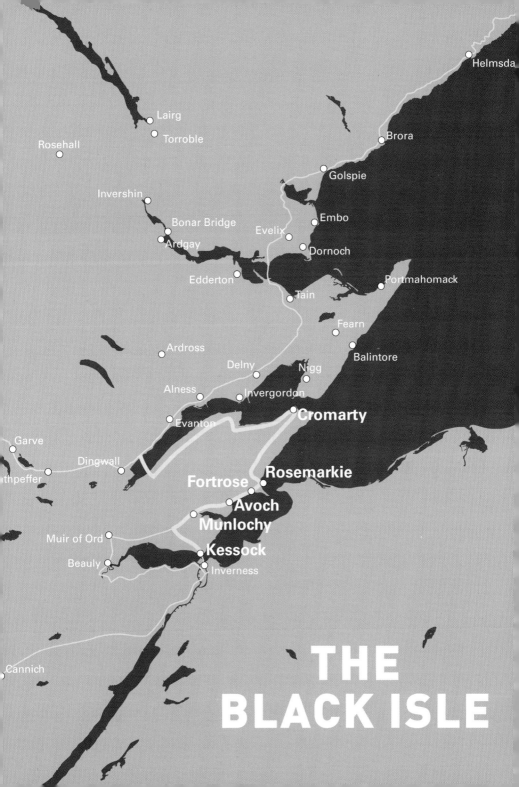

THE
BLACK ISLE

Bottlenose dolphin leaping for salmon at Chanonry Point

ORD ARMS HOTEL, Muir of Ord

STAY
£

A small and intimate, family-owned hotel accommodation in the heart of the Black Isle, just a 10-minute walk from the small village of Muir of Ord. The hotel itself dates back over 100 years to 1904.

Nearby sights include the Singleton Distillery, just 10 minutes by foot, where you can sample some of the Black Isle's famous whisky selection. The beaches of Rosemarkie and Fortrose are also just a 20-minute drive away, both of which are a popular spot for dolphin, porpoise, and seal spotting.
///unto.condensed.climbing

NORTH KESSOCK HOTEL, Kessock

EAT &
STAY
£££

Facing south over the peaceful waters of the Beauly Firth, the North Kessock Hotel is just a short drive from the city centre of Inverness, yet feels like a whole other world. Once the landing point of the Kessock ferry, the small harbour has played a significant role in the history and conflicts in the region.

Over the years, the size and number of ferries increased, until the Kessock Bridge was built in 1980, when demand for the crossing became too great. Since then, the old Kessock Ferry Inn changed to the North Kessock Hotel and became one of the finest hotel accommodations in the area and has welcomed visitors to the beautiful shores of the Black Isle ever since.
///buggy.wonderfully.latched

WHITE COTTAGE FOOD AND ACCOMMODATION, Kessock

EAT &
STAY
£

Once home to the ferrymen of Kessock and their families, this small stone cottage has been converted into a beautiful hotel and restaurant on the banks of the Beauly Firth.

As well as serving up a range of foods and a selection of freshly baked goods, the White Cottage is also proud to support the local RNLI service. For each purchase of fish and chips from the restaurant, a donation will be made to the lifeboat service to support their hard work in the region.
///octagon.calculate.notched

BLACK ISLE PODS AND CHALET, Munlochy

Tucked away in the Black Isle countryside near Fortrose, is the Black Isle Pods and Chalet. These medium-sized units are cosy and extremely comfortable with a large couch, that doubles as a sofa bed, and a double bed. This self-catering accommodation has a small kitchenette and dining area; on arrival you will receive a welcome pack with breakfast items and tasty nibbles. At time of booking there is also the option to add on a breakfast meat package for you to enjoy during your stay.

The owners, Audrey and Frank, have really thought about everything when it comes to a comfortable night away. There is a shed outside with a fridge and freezer where you can purchase pizza, Black Isle ice-cream and soft drinks.

The highlight feature of this accommodation is the fire pit and hot tub outside of your pod. This is the perfect way to wind down after a day of exploring the highlands.
///orbited.rezoning.offline

ALLANGRANGE HOTEL, Munlochy

Overlooking the beautiful natural sand basin of Munlochy Bay sits the small village of Munlochy. This quiet village began to grow in size around the middle of the 18th century when it was used to house workers quarrying stone for the construction of Fort George, which can still be seen today on the opposite side of the Moray Firth.

The Allangrange Hotel offers a warm and welcoming stay to guests and also provides warm and hearty meals to those wishing to dine in, as well as take food away. The hotel offers the choice of five boutique rooms, equipped with all of the amenities you need for a comfortable trip, from a hairdryer to a TV. Each room also comes with a complimentary light breakfast, so you don't need to worry about going hungry before your big day out on the NC500.
///denim.tender.outlined

HARBOUR FISH AND CHIPS, Avoch

EAT
£

Just a short walk from the peaceful setting of Avoch Harbour, this traditional British fish and chip shop serves up delicious and fresh seafood, as well as pizzas and kebabs, for a very reasonable price. With no dine-in options, this take-away is the perfect stop-off as you head through the Black Isle if you fancy a warming chip-shop dinner with a view.

We recommend heading north to Rosemarkie Bay to enjoy dinner with a view across the water to Fort George and beyond out to the North Sea.
///throwaway.newspaper.combining

BAKHOOS BAKERY, Fortrose

EAT
£££

Bakhoose Bakery was established in 2021 and is an incredibly popular business in the area of Fortrose. Using Scottish-grown and milled flours, the speciality at Bakhoose Bakery is their sourdough.

In addition to this freshly baked bread, they also offer a unique cake selection along with pastries and coffee. It is recommended to visit early in the day to enjoy the freshly baked goods as they are likely to sell out fast. Bakhoose Bakery is located on the High Street in Fortrose and has a small amount of parking outside.
///whirlwind.yacht.wanted

WATER'S EDGE, Fortrose

STAY
£££

A 5-star B&B that sits overlooking the Moray Firth just a short walk from the small village of Fortrose. This beautifully secluded accommodation consists of three double bedrooms on the first floor, each fitted with en-suite facilities, a large and comfortable bed, and a private balcony to enjoy the stunning view of the water.

From arrival all the way to departure, a stay at the Water's Edge is an experience to remember, with a guaranteed warm and friendly welcome and a beautiful setting to relax in during your visit to the highlands.
///goose.streamers.rapid

Bakhoos Bakery, Inverness

FORTROSE CARAVAN PARK, Fortrose

STAY £

Walking distance from the historic town of Fortrose, the Fortrose Caravan Park is perfectly situated for those wishing to experience the best of the Black Isle. Perched on the shoreline of the natural sand bar that is known as Chanonry Point, this campsite is in close proximity to the famous golf course, and one of Scotland's best viewpoints for dolphin spotting.

The caravan park itself sits on the southern side of Chanonry Point and has space for 50 pitches with electric hookups, as well as two toilet blocks, a kitchen, and laundry facilities. It is also perfect for dog owners as the site is dog-friendly and is the perfect location for long walks along the seaside.
///hello.pelt.unlimited

THE 19TH RESTAURANT, Fortrose

EAT ££

A friendly, warm welcome awaits you at the Fortrose and Rosemarkie Golf Club where you can sit and enjoy the views with a tasty meal from the local menu. This golf club opened in 1793, making it the 15th oldest golf course in the world and there is lots of interesting history that you can learn from your visit.

The food that is prepared here is all local produce, the fresh bread comes straight from the Cromarty Bakery and the fish comes in fresh from Tain.
///pleaser.segregate.sunflower

ROSEMARKIE CAMPING AND CARAVANNING CLUB CAMPSITE, Fortrose

STAY £££

Rosemarkie Camping and Caravan Club Campsite overlooks the Moray Firth and is only a 10 minute walk from Chanonry Point, a popular spot to see dolphins. The campsite features pitches with electric hook ups, as well as those without alongside many other great onsite facilities. The site is open to non-members of the Caravan Club and also invites tourers, tents and motorhomes to enjoy this campsite.

The campsite is withing walking distance of a number of great cafes and restaurants, as well as the Fortrose and Rosemarkie Golf Club which sits at the end of the peninsula. Rosemarkie Beach is a popular location for those who enjoy wild swimming, families with young children and dog walkers as the beach is dog-friendly all year round.

///ballooned.navigate.compress

CROFTERS CAFE, Rosemarkie

A beachfront cafe located in Rosemarkie serving a delicious variety of foods, from burgers to seafood and a good selection of vegetarian and vegan options. We recommend their vegan burger and the chips are incredible too! The specials board displays the soup of the day as well as the wine special and other delicacies on offer.

Enjoy your meal inside the atmospheric cafe area with windows looking out to Rosemarkie beach or in the open beer garden area outside.

Crofters Cafe is open for breakfast, serving daily from 10am. This is perfect if you are staying the night in their studio accommodation and are looking for a bite to eat in the morning.

If you are after something sweet, don't hesitate to try one of their delicious cakes or tiffins or try their caramel-filled churros or Nutella® pancakes.

///desks.sharpness.runs

The chef serves up a feast at Crofters Cafe, Rosemarkie

EAT &
STAY
££

ROYAL HOTEL, Cromarty

This beautiful hotel was taken over by a local of Cromarty in 2010 and since then has offered a peaceful escape with exceptional highland hospitality. With each of the bedrooms in the Royal Hotel set to a different layout and style, each visit to the Royal Hotel will be unique and enjoyable.

As well as being a peaceful and relaxing location, Cromarty is also the perfect place to explore the coastline by boat with the local company Ecoventure.
///tweed.variation.ramp

STAY
££

NC5OO

SUTOR COOPS LODGES, Cromarty

Luxury cabins in the heart of the ancient Black Isle. The Sutor Coops lodges are a set of twin glamping lodges overlooking the small town of Cromarty, offering stunning views of the Croamrty Firth and beyond.

All entirely self-catering, offering onsite parking, free WIFI, BBQ facilities, and a complete kitchen with all of the utensils you will need for a relaxing and enjoyable stay. To top it all off, guests at the Sutor Coops lodges can enjoy the luxury of a private hot tub with views of the stunning Scottish highlands.
///achieving.racing.cookbooks

EAT
££

SUTOR CREEK CAFE, Cromarty

Sutor Creek is a licenced deli and take-away serving up the most delicious wood-fired pizzas and cooked food to take away, located on the Cromarty Harbour. The locally sourced produce is served inline with the season and features the best of the Black Isle.

As well as offering cooked food, the deli is stocked up with tasty local produce from around the Black Isle.
///testing.quibble.comedians

NEWHALL MAINS, Dingwall

Newhall Mains is a beautiful family-run property in the Dingwall region of the Scottish Highlands. This boutique hotel opened in 2020 after being restored and has five spacious cottages and four double rooms. There is also an Old Coach House which is self-contained on the land.

Newhall Mains is the only luxury accommodation in the UK with its own airfield, providing easy access for arrivals or simple entertainment to those with interest in aviation. The restaurant is also open to the public and offers an intimate and memorable dining experience, just make sure to call ahead as space is limited and private functions are common.
///roadways.herb.cried

EAT & STAY £££

THE COTTAGE BAR AND RESTAURANT, Dingwall

A place for those in search of traditional Scottish cuisine, made with seasonal and local produce and served up with passion and care.

After the community of Maryburgh welcomed the takeover of the Cottage Bar and Restaurant with such open arms, this venue has strived to become an integral part of the local community. The Cottage has shown its gratitude by supporting the Maryburgh Amenties Hall, as well as the local men's shed, and are even sponsors of the Maryburgh Football Team. Eating and drinking at the Cottage Bar and Restaurant, therefore, not only be a treat for the senses, it will also help to support the local community. A real win-win!
///inch.televise.frostbite

EAT & STAY ££

NC500

Tarbat Ness Lighthouse, Tain

BATTY'S BAPS, Dingwall

The perfect small cafe for a quick, grab-and-go breakfast or lunch, Batty's Baps can be found in the town centre of Dingwall serving up delicious home-cooked and hearty foods to set you up for a full day of exploring. With sit-in or take-away options, the friendly staff at this small cafe are always ready to welcome you through the door and help you to enjoy your visit to the highlands of Scotland.

///cook.wells.triathlon

CHILLI MASALA, Dingwall

Chilli Masala is a top-quality Indian restaurant on the east coast of the NC500, offering delicious authentic Indian cuisine in the Scottish Highlands. Paul and Faysol are partners in Chilli Masala and aim to ensure that customers not only enjoy a great meal but experience a friendly and welcoming service.

///retina.wreck.blues

DINGWALL CAMPING AND CARAVANNING CLUB, Dingwall

Situated at the very end of the Cromarty Firth, ideally placed right beside the town of Dingwall, this campsite is a fantastic option for those travelling by public transport or for anyone looking for a campsite with easy access to bars and restaurants.

With around 70 pitches, including a mixture of grass and hard-standing pitches, as well as electrical hookups, this campsite is perfect for all campers, from campervans to tents. The site also has a shower block that is praised for its cleanliness, accessible facilities, washbasins, and an onsite shop for essentials.

///calculate.typist.mushroom

TULLOCH CASTLE, Dingwall

Dating back to the 12th century, Tulloch Castle has a lively history and has been listed as a finalist in the Scottish Castle awards. The castle's charm has been retained over the years, including the Great Hall which dates back 250 years.

Today, this stunning building welcomes guests to the Scottish highlands to stay in one of the 22 unique bedrooms or to dine in the dungeon.
///vintages.recur.dined

EAT
££

ROSEMOUNT COTTAGE AND BOTHY, Garve

Located on the banks of the Black Water river, Rosemount Cottage and Bothy are self-catering accommodations that can be booked individually or together. The Cottage sleeps four and The Bothy can sleep up to four with the use of the sofa bed.

John and Helen Forteith recently renovated both cottages, which date back to the 1850s, ensuring that guests are provided with a comfortable and relaxing experience, while maintaining many of the special period features.

Rosemount Cottage and Bothy is an ideal location for exploring the NC500.
///deciding.topical.crumbles

EAT &
STAY
££

BEN WYVIS HOTEL, Strathpeffer

The Ben Wyvis Hotel is located in the centre of the beautiful Victorian spa town of Strathpeffer. The hotel was purpose-built for use as a hotel, opening in 1879 and was extended in 1864, however, it was used as a hospital during the first world war.

A warm welcome awaits you at this charming hotel which has a variety of rooms including a honeymoon suite with stunning views across the gardens. The restaurant serves locally sourced Scottish food which is influenced by seasonality and features a carvery every Sunday.

Ben Wyvis Hotel is surrounded by five acres of woods with stunning views of the munro, Ben Wyvis itself.
///nickname.shunning.carpets

Coul House

COUL HOUSE HOTEL, Strathpeffer

You can expect a friendly welcome when you enter Coul House which is owned by Stuart and Susannah, who also help to operate the hotel and restaurant on a day-to-day basis. This stunning mansion dates back to the 1820s and has external castle-like features making it feel extremely mystical.

Local chef Garry cooks up the most delicious food and great wine is served alongside it at Coul House. The hotel's open-door policy will see the team aiming to squeeze anyone in to enjoy the atmosphere of this magnificent 18th century building.

There are a range of different bedrooms throughout the hotel to suit your needs and a comfortable lounge area and bar. Enjoy a walk in the beautiful gardens where guests of all ages enjoy the fairy trail and the surrounding woods. Coul House is the perfect stay on the NC500 route, located a 25 minute drive outside of Inverness.
///cheater.signed.craziest

BLACKROCK CARAVAN PARK, Evanton

Cathy and Gary welcome you to their campsite located in the village of Evanton in the beautiful Glen Glass. The Blackrock Caravan Park sits only one mile away from the A9 making it very convenient for those travelling the NC500 road trip. The caravan park was named after the nearby Black Rock Gorge, a 120-foot deep gorge that was carved out by the River Glass.

A short walk from the Blackrock Caravan Park is a local shop as well as a village pub selling great food. As well as being a caravan park, there are also pods on site.
///cassettes.leave.presented

KILTEARN GUEST HOUSE, Evanton

EAT & STAY £££

A great place to stop off on your adventure is Kiltearn Guest House. This 4-star hotel has won awards in its service and accommodation, with exceptionally friendly and welcoming staff and luxurious accommodation options to make you feel right at home.

Set in a 19th-century, former Victorian manse, Kiltearn Guest House is located in a beautiful countryside setting overlooking the Cromarty Firth. Ideally located just a short drive from the A9, this is a popular resting place for those exploring the NC500 as it lies right in the middle of the eastern seaboard fishing villages and the towering mountain of Ben Wyvis to the west. It's an ideal place for those wishing to spend time exploring this beautiful region of Scotland.
///flexibly.alternate.timed

THE STOREHOUSE, Evanton

EAT £

The Storehouse restaurant, deli, and gift shop sits on the northern banks of the Cromarty Firth, just off the A9. This popular stop-off not only serves up a mouthwatering selection of meals and home baking, the deli and gift shop also stock a wide selection of local produce and crafts from the surrounding area.

On a sunny day, the Storehouse offers an outdoor seating area with beautiful views of the Cromarty Firth, perfect for a relaxing coffee with a view. Just keep your eyes peeled for some of the local seals that are often spotted along the shoreline.
///daffodils.grid.herds

The little car ferry which crosses the Cromarty Firth between Cromarty and Nigg

BEECHWOOD LODGE, Ardross

EAT
££

Beechwood Lodge is a stunning guest house near Alness where you can feel relaxed in a peaceful environment. Gunta and Kristine are the mother and daughter duo that will go the extra mile to welcome you into their home along with their two friendly dogs and a cat. This beautiful house has five bedrooms with views overlooking the fields for ultimate tranquillity.

If you are looking to book a trip to the highlands that consists of little self-planning but a lot of adventure, you can book a package at the Beechwood Lodge. This consists of sitting down with Gunta and Kristine and personalising your itinerary for your weekend away.
///flip.boss.accordion

KINCRAIG CASTLE, Invergordon

EAT &
STAY
£££

What better way is there to make your trip to Scotland one to remember than a stay in a 17th-century castle overlooking the beautiful Cromarty Firth and the mystical Black Isle? Kincraig Castle has been home to the Mackenzie Clan, one of Scotland's most well-known and powerful clans, for generations. Today, it serves as one of Scotland's most luxurious accommodation settings, and is an award-winning 4-star country house.
The grand country house of Kincraig sits on 10 acres of land, giving plenty of room to stretch your legs and explore the beautiful landscape and forests of Easter Ross. It also has an onsite restaurant that is open to the public, offering an extravagant menu of locally produced meat, vegetables, and freshly caught seafood.

If you are looking for a more unique dining experience, Kincraig Castle also offers handcrafted picnic and afternoon tea picnic experiences. These on-the-go meals are expertly crafted by the experienced chefs at Kincraig and are perfect for a more luxurious hiking lunch or seaside snack.
///trimmer.amaze.treatable

EAT &
STAY
££

SHANDWICK INN, Invergordon

A simple, comfortable and cosy hotel with an onsite bar and restaurant that offers a range of traditional Scottish meals, the Shandwick Inn is a popular stopping point in the Easter Ross region. The Inn is noted for its large portions of food and friendly and welcoming staff.

Nearby sights include the seaboard towns of Balintore and Portmahomack, as well as the ancient and mysterious Shandwick Stone and the Tarbat Ness Lighthouse.
///belly.dice.nuzzling

EAT &
STAY
££

THE SHIP INN, Invergordon

A charming boutique-style hotel in the heart of the industrial seaside town of Invergordon. The Ship Inn features a warm and welcoming interior with big windows and wooden flooring, giving the hotel itself a nautical feel. There are a total of 12 rooms, all decorated to a high standard, with big windows and plenty of natural light.

The restaurant is open to the public seven days a week and offers an extensive range of delicious Scottish food that is updated frequently, all freshly sourced and homemade onsite. Due to the high popularity of the Ship Inn's restaurant, it is highly recommended that you book in advance to avoid disappointment.
///promotion.sweep.motivates

EAT &
STAY
£

TUCKERS INN, Invergordon

If you are looking for beautiful views over the Cromarty Firth, Tuckers Inn can provide you with that from its conservatory dining room and newly refurbished en-suite bedrooms. Single, double and family rooms are available at an affordable price.

Located on the seafront in Invergordon, this hotel gives you a great base for exploring the local surroundings such as distilleries or castles.
///condense.diverting.pylons

The harbour, Portmahomack

WHITE ROSE TOWER, Invergordon

The White Rose Tower is a luxury accommodation for adults to enjoy some peace and tranquillity from the modern-day hustle and bustle. The exterior of the White Rose Tower resembles a castle and some of the rooms are located at the top of a spiral staircase where WIFI and mobile signals may be weak. The interior is very tasteful and all of the rooms have been uniquely decorated with bespoke furnishings.

The White Rose Tower is the perfect place to retreat on the NC500, surrounded as it is by woodland tranquillity. With friendly staff and a comfortable bed to rest your head, it is guaranteed that a warm welcome awaits you at the White Rose Tower.

///perfume.merely.defensive

DELNY GLAMPING, Delny

On the northern coast of the Cromarty Firth is a glamping site that has a range of unique accommodations, all for a very reasonable price. During your stay at the Delny Glamping site, you can choose from the custom-made whisky barrel pods, the slightly larger, two bedroom "highland bothies", or the latest addition to the site, a former salmon smokehouse nicknamed "The Auld Reekie".

If you fancy something a little more "bricks and mortar", there is also a self-catering apartment, which is attached to the main house and dates back to the 16th century.

The entire site is ideal for families, designed and built to be a safe and secure setting for young kids. Surrounding the glamping site you will find a large forestry area with plenty of walking tracks to explore, a petting zoo with chickens, pigs, and pygmy goats that you can meet and feed, and an onsite playpark to keep the kids entertained while you relax.

///fermented.chuckle.firewall

DELNY HIGHLAND LODGES, Delny

Set among the tranquil woodlands of Easter Ross, the Delny Highland Lodges offer a countryside escape for the family with large and luxurious wooden lodges. All of the lodges here come fully equipped with kitchen facilities and utensils, and have access to the facilities such as the children's playpark, the nearby Loch Katrine for boat hire and fishing, and the cosy pub.

The park also offers activities such as horse riding, fly fishing and cycle hire, and is located close to the beautiful beaches on the eastern seaboard of Easter Ross. Perfect for a family getaway or romantic couples' retreat.
///estuaries.subsets.passes

CASTLE CRAIG CLIFFTOPS, Nigg

Stunning self-catering pods overlooking the Cromarty Firth are waiting for you at Castle Craig Clifftops. Book a pod for a romantic getaway or a larger one for a break with your family and enjoy the tranquillity and views from your private hot tub. The decor inside the pods is very modern, with home-from-home luxuries such as a dishwasher and WIFI.

A welcome hamper with locally sourced produce and tea and coffee is waiting for your arrival.
///choppers.plant.dozens

PITCALZEAN HOUSE, Nigg

This Georgian House is the perfect place for a family getaway in the highlands. Pitcalzean House is nestled in 33 acres of nature, the entrance to the house showing off beautiful views of the Cromarty Firth and the Black Isle, and is only a 40 minute drive from the highland capital, Inverness.

This mansion sleeps 18 guests with the option of increasing it to 36 for larger parties. The charming interior features a large living room and library area, a spacious dining room and entertainment rooms with activities such as a snooker table.

Pitcalzean House, Nigg

The local area has plenty to do, with Tain being the nearest town and Dornoch Beach being a beautiful nearby stretch of sand. The Royal Dornoch Golf Course is also only a 30 minute drive away.
///unsettled.solar.rice

BALINTORE INN, Balintore

EAT & STAY ££

With beachside views and a short trip to the Scottish mountains, the town of Balintore is an undiscovered gem on the NC500 coastal route. This quiet fishing village is home to attractions such as the Mermaid of the North, a 10ft bronze statue that is often swallowed up by the sea; the Pictish Stone, a 9ft slab of stone carved hundreds of years ago by the mysterious Picts; and of course, the warm welcome of the Balintore Inn.

Sitting right on the seaside overlooking the beach, this cosy hotel, bar and restaurant is the perfect place to call home for the night if you are looking to explore the region of Easter Ross. The hotel features a terraced area, where guests can enjoy the views over the beach, as well as an onsite bar and restaurant, with log fires for the cold Scottish winters and outdoor seating for the beautiful summer days.
///riverbank.deeds.dugouts

GLENMORANGIE HOUSE, Fearn

EAT & STAY £££

An accommodation that will give you an exceptional experience on your visit to the Scottish Highlands, this boutique hotel invites you to enjoy a stay in one of its bespoke bedrooms which are uniquely decorated.

Whilst you are there, you may wish to book yourself a tour at the Glenmorangie Distillery where you can try some of the delicious flavours of whisky distilled here. Crafting single malt whisky since 1843, the Glenmorangie Distillery is one of the most famous and reputable distilleries in the highlands of Scotland.
///dumpy.galloping.aquatics

NC500

THE CASTLE HOTEL, Portmahomack

Situated in the small fishing village of Portmahomack, the Castle Hotel offers the chance to stay in one of the NC500's most peaceful and underappreciated regions. This small fishing village is a unique setting in the highlands of Scotland as it is the only westerly facing town on the east coast, meaning beautiful sunsets over the distant hills, and it is also situated in one of the driest areas in Scotland, meaning it is perfect for a seaside getaway.

The Castle Hotel has four comfortable and cosy bedrooms, two of which offer stunning sea views over the Dornoch Firth and beyond. The bar and restaurant has a local feel to it, with live music events, a good selection of whisky, and a variety of locally crafted beers from Orkney, Cromarty, and the Black Isle.
///obstruct.future.blues

THE OYSTER CATCHER, Portmahomack

A small, intimate and high-quality seafood restaurant on the main street of the small town of Portmahomack that also features a Bed and Breakfast with three rooms for those wishing to spend the night. This unique restaurant offers a fixed menu of the finest ingredients and local cuisine, served with a range of tasters to make the experience of dining here one to remember.

The bar at the Oyster Catcher also features a large whisky menu known as the Malt Vault, with a wide range of both international spirits and, of course, local Scottish whiskies from across the country.
///toys.kidney.houseboat

PORTMAHOMACK CAMPSITE, Portmahomack

A small campsite overlooking the southern shores of the Dornoch Firth, the Portmahomack Campsite sits just outside of the beautiful fishing village of Portmahomack. With only 35 pitches onsite, this campsite is perfect for those seeking a quiet and relaxing escape from the busier side of life.

The Mermaid of the North, Balintore

In the town of Portmahomack, you will find shops and a cosy pub, as well as a possibility of seeing dolphins playing in the firth to the north. Nearby, you will also find the magnificent Portmahomack Church, which is partially funded by the profits of the campsite.
///hurtles.gazette.bundles

STAY
£

DORNOCH FIRTH CARAVAN PARK, Tain
Dornoch Firth Caravan Park is located a short drive away from the small town of Dornoch, overlooking the Dornoch Firth. There are pitches with electric hook-ups available for caravans and motorhomes and a separate level area for tents. There are great laundry facilities on site, as well as unisex and accessible bathrooms.

The Dornoch Firth Caravan Park is within walking distance of the Meikle Ferry Station restaurant.
///relished.swing.sparkles

STAY
££

MANSFIELD CASTLE HOTEL, Tain
Set on three acres of beautiful, picturesque countryside, Mansfield Castle is a luxurious accommodation just a short walk from the historical town of Tain, Scotland's oldest royal burgh (dating back to 1066). The castle itself was built in the 1870s and sits proudly overlooking the Dornoch Firth with its distinct and recognisable towers.

Mansfield Castle has 19 beautifully decorated rooms, as well as an onsite bar and restaurant serving award-winning food. The castle is ideally located for the wide range of nearby activities that Easter Ross has to offer, including golf, fishing, and exploring the nearby town of Tain.
///bluffing.noise.stones

EAT &
STAY
££

MEIKLE FERRY STATION, Tain
On the site of the old railway station at what is now the Dornoch Firth Bridge, the Meikle Ferry station is a family friendly and extremely welcoming cafe, restaurant, and accommodation

complex. After recently going through an extensive refurbishment, the staff at the old train station aim to make any and all visitors feel at home, from locals to tourists alike.

The original building of the Meikle Ferry Station dates back to 1864 when it was used as a final station on the route north. Within five years, however, the station was closed down as the railway was extended further west towards Bonar Bridge.

After this, the building served as the Meikle Ferry Inn as the main ferry crossing to Dornoch left from here. That, of course, came to an end in 1991 when the Dornoch Firth Bridge was built and the ferry was no longer required.

As with most things in the north of Scotland, times change and yet the culture and heritage is always remembered. With this, the Meikle Ferry Station name was retained to remember the important role this building played in the surrounding area. ///backtrack.drive.makeovers

MORANGIE HOTEL, Tain
Situated in one of Scotland's oldest burghs, Tain, the old Victorian Mansion, known as the Morangie Hotel, is renowned for its spacious and comfortable rooms, as well as its delicious and home-cooked meals.

The Morangie Hotel was built at the beginning of the 20th century, funded by the success of the tea trade between India and Great Britain at that time. The Victorian tea-planter, Joshua Taylor, left much of his wealth to his two nieces, one of whom used her share of the fortune to build this fine mansion in the highlands of Scotland.

Today, the hotel is synonymous with comfort and class, with its beautifully leafy gardens and scenic views over the quaint town of Tain. The rooms are all bright and airy, recently refurbished to a tasteful and modern decor, whilst still maintaining the class that one would expect in the original building.

EAT & STAY ££

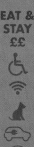

Mansfield Castle Hotel, Tain

As with other establishments in Tain, the Morangie Hotel is ideally situated for reaching activities from Inverness up to Sutherland, and everything in between.
///blanking.mugs.putter

PLATFORM 1864, Tain

EAT
££

A unique restaurant located in Tain is Platform 1864. The old railway station was converted into a bistro in 2015, led by Graham, the owner and chef with the aim of restoring the building and keeping it alive.

The restaurant features parts of the old railway such as railway tracks lining the bottom of the bar area. The interior is quirky and modern and you will receive a warm welcome when you stop by for a meal or a coffee and cake. Platform 1864 is open for breakfast, lunch and dinner throughout the week and serves a great variety of delicious meals, sourcing their produce from local suppliers.
///spenders.lifted.sliders

ROYAL TAIN HOTEL, Tain

STAY
££

Situated in the heart of Scotland's oldest royal burgh, the Royal Tain Hotel is a beautiful French Gothic manor building constructed in 1872. This listed building has maintained its beautiful exterior look whilst the interior has undergone a tasteful and modern refurbishment to all 25 en-suite rooms.

The reputation of the Royal Tain Hotel is one of a place of fine-dining and comfortable accommodation with excellent service, all for a very reasonable price. The restaurant utilises fresh and locally sourced ingredients to produce a delicious range of traditional Scottish meals.

The Royal Tain Hotel proves to be a popular location for visitors to the region thanks to its convenient location in Tain town centre, as well as the nearby sights and activities, such as the Glenmorangie Distillery, the Tain Golf Course, the Royal Dornoch Golf Club, and the beautiful Dunrobin Castle.
///multiply.gent.prefect

SHANDWICK HOUSE, Tain

A cosy guesthouse set in a restored 19th century building near to the beautiful expanse of water known as the Dornoch Firth. Shandwick House consists of a collection of six rooms, each with a private bathroom, a TV, electric kettle, and an exceptional Scottish breakfast included with the room each morning.

This guest house is a highly popular choice for couples looking for a romantic town-centre getaway and is fantastic value for money.
///mistaken.optimally.reviews

WILLIAM GRANT BAKERY, Tain

The William Grant Bakery has won many awards for its pies over the years and it is highly regarded in the town of Tain. This takeaway bakery has the last traditional scotch oven in the north of Scotland. As well as selling pies, we also recommend trying the fresh bread and cakes that are baked daily at the William Grant Bakery.
///jolt.scam.childcare

Platform 1864, Tain

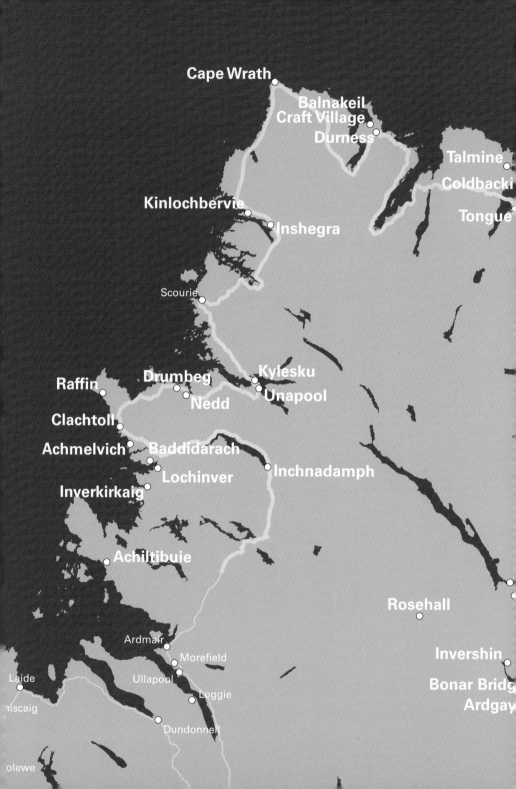

Dunnet
Head

Brough

Mey

Scrabster

Upper

Castletown

Forss

Thurso

Ke

Armadale

Strathy

Melvich

Bettyhill

Borgie

Halkirk

SUTHERLAND

Wick

Puldagon

Thru

Lybster

Latheron

Dunbeath

Berriedale

Helmsdale

Brora

ble

Golspie

Embo

Evelix

Dornoch

derton

Portmahomack

Tain

Puffins on Handa Island, Sutherland

COACH HOUSE BAR AND RESTAURANT, Dornoch

EAT
££

This bar and restaurant overlooks the main square of Dornoch town and is the perfect spot to stop off for a quick drink and bite to eat, or a full dining-in experience. The owners of the Coach House are the local Mackay family who also own the local butcher shop and farmland surround Dornoch, meaning you can be assured that all of the meat on the menu is as fresh and locally sourced as it comes.

The well-stocked bar is also open seven days a week and is very popular with the locals of Dornoch, with beautiful views over the bustling high street and on to the impressive outline of Dornoch Cathedral. Try a dram of the local whisky and relax as the world passes you by in this highland town.
///unwanted.bookings.countries

COCOA MOUNTAIN, Dornoch

EAT
£££

An iconic cafe on the North Coast 500 route is the decadent chocolate cafe, Cocoa Mountain. Staff here craft their own artisan chocolates, full of different flavours and textures that are a highlight for anyone visiting the area. Cocoa Mountain has two cafes on the route, one is Dornoch on the east coast and one in Balnakeil on the north coast.

We adore their hot chocolate which is made using their melted chocolate and full-cream milk. Plant milks are also available for those with specific dietary requirements, however, it is worth noting that the hot chocolate itself still contains milk.
///followers.tweezers.squeaking

DORNOCH BEACH CAMPSITE, Dornoch

STAY
££

Set on the spectacular stretch of sand of Dornoch Beach, the Dornoch Beach Campsite offers one of the best views in the region. As one of the longest and arguably most beautiful beaches on the NC500, Dornoch Beach has been given a Seaside Award status due to its clean water and easy access for swimming and sunbathing.

The campsite sits among the sand dunes that border the beach, with 120 pitches spanning its 25 acre site. There is a shop for essentials, a laundrette and washing up facility, free showers, and also a games room and children's play area.
///helpfully.earth.carriage

DORNOCH CASTLE, Dornoch

Located right in the heart of the historic town of Dornoch, this 16th century castle has been fully renovated to now offer a unique accommodation option, perfectly situated on the NC500 route. With 24 different rooms, as well as an onsite restaurant, walled garden, and beautiful views of the 12th century cathedral across the road, Dornoch Castle is the perfect place to stay for those wishing to explore the town of Dornoch and the region of Easter Ross in more depth.

Guests can choose from a range of rooms, from the standard selection in the modern extension of the castle, to the deluxe range in the oldest section of the castle, which are all complete with four-poster beds, original stonework on the walls, and a spa bath and shower.
///ruby.toasters.outlines

DORNOCH HOTEL, Dornoch

Sitting just a short walk from the centre of the historic town of Dornoch, the Dornoch Hotel is one of the largest in the area with over 100 rooms, two onsite restaurants, a bar, and, of course, spectacular views of Dornoch Beach and the open ocean. The rooms available at this impressive hotel range from large family rooms to standard twin rooms, perfect for all travellers.
///signified.charcoal.paramedic

THE EAGLE HOTEL, Dornoch

The Eagle Hotel is a central accommodation within the highland town of Dornoch on the east coast of the NC500. There are a number of bedrooms suitable for solo travellers or those travelling as a family. The rooms include a flat screen TV and a desk and all rooms have an en-suite bathroom.

Dornoch Castle Hotel, Dornoch

The Eagle Hotel is Dornoch's first and only bar with hotel rooms so if this is something that you enjoy then this is a great hotel for you. They have an impressive whisky selection that you can enjoy, alongside a delicious meal from the restaurant which serves locally sourced highland produce.

The Eagle Hotel is a great base for exploring the sights on the east coast of the NC500.
///riverbed.stocks.veered

EAT
£££

THE HIGHLAND LARDER, Dornoch
The Highland Larder is an outdoor kiosk located on the banks of Dornoch Beach beside the Dornoch Caravan and Camping Park. The speciality served here is seafood, however they also serve cakes and hot drinks at the Highland Larder. There are picnic benches outside the kiosk or you are only a short walk to Dornoch Beach if you would rather eat your food with a sea view.
///parrot.boosted.protected

EAT &
STAY
£££

NC5❍O

LINKS HOUSE HOTEL AT ROYAL DORNOCH, Dornoch
Incredible luxury right in the heart of the historic town of Dornoch, the Links House Hotel takes comfort to the next level. This 5-star hotel sits overlooking the open stretch of land of the Dornoch Golf Course and boasts stunning views of the golden sands of Dornoch Beach. The main building of the hotel dates back to 1843 and has retained the beautiful details of the craftsmanship of this era, with intricate details on the walls, roof, and even the doors.

Originally, this building was used to house the minister for the local church, however, in 2011, it was opened as a hotel. Soon after, in 2013, a second building was constructed to match the style of the original, increasing the number of rooms available for guests. Despite its new age, this addition has been created with incredible attention to detail to ensure it matches the style of the original building.

The hotel contains a luxurious communal lounge for guests and

the public to enjoy, featuring open fireplaces and an honesty bar in the luxurious lounge area. The onsite restaurant, the MARA, offers a wide range of locally produced food, aiming to keep as much of the sourcing as possible within 80 miles of Dornoch.
///apes.quality.rebounded

ROYAL GOLF HOTEL, Dornoch

Sitting high up on the banks of Dornoch Beach, the Royal Golf Hotel in Dornoch boasts unspoiled views of the miles of golden sand that stretch along the eastern coast of Sutherland. This 4-star hotel sits right on the first tee of the world-famous Dornoch Golf Course, hence the name, making it the perfect hotel for those wishing to practice golf in the highlands of the sport's home country.

The hotel features a range of rooms and self-catering apartments, some with spectacular views of the golf course and sea views beyond. Each of the rooms and suites is decorated to the highest standard and is set to guarantee a comfortable and memorable stay here in Dornoch.
///failed.remembers.paving

EVELIX PODS, Evelix

Set just off of the main road north in Scotland, the Evelix Pods offers a selection of six different glamping pods, all guaranteed to please. Combining all that the highlands of Scotland has to offer, from the stunning mountain views to the nearby beaches, the Evelix Pods are highly rated across all of the world's top booking platforms, and it is easy to see why.

All of the pods in Evelix come with heated flooring, kitchen facilities, private decking, and a highland welcome (combined with a very thoughtful welcome pack). It is also situated nicely just a 5-minute walk from the nearest licensed restaurant, and is just a short drive from the historic town of Dornoch.
///police.looms.shower

Carbisdale Castle, near Bonar Bridge

DRUMBHAN CARAVAN CLUB SITE, Ardgay

This small campsite can be found just to the north of the small town of Bonar Bridge, far from the busy main roads in the region. It is a peaceful site with just five pitches for touring vehicles, all with electric hookups, and enjoys stunning views to the south of Loch Migdale, the Kyle of Sutherland and further on to Ben Wyvis.

Due to its westward location from the busy main route of the A9, the area surrounding Drumbhan and out towards the beautiful Falls of Shin is often undiscovered by those visiting the region.

///totals.hydration.oppose

STAY
£

CAIRN POD GLAMPING, Bonar Bridge

Situated in Bonar Bridge, Cairn Pod Glamping is a great location for exploring the NC500. This eco-friendly pod is fully insulated and comes complete with a comfortable bed, wet room and small kitchen area, making it a comfortable place to stay when you are visiting the Scottish Highlands. The site also has safe bicycle storage.

Incredible panoramic views can be enjoyed from the outdoor seating area, which also includes a gas BBQ. A complimentary cold continental breakfast is supplied at the Cairn Pod.

///emptied.less.croaking

STAY
£

INVERSHIN HOTEL BUNKHOUSE AND BAR, Invershin

As the road leaves the coastline of Sutherland, passing through Bonar Bridge and winding along the banks of the Kyle of Sutherland, the welcoming sight of the Invershin Hotel sits by the roadside, ready to show highland hospitality to any and all travellers. The hotel overlooks the tranquil waters of the Kyle and beyond to the distant outline of the beautiful Carbisdale Castle, offering a peaceful retreat to the highlands away from the busy cities to the south.

Inside the hotel you will find a restaurant and bar, as well as a range of rooms for guests to spend the night in, ranging from bunkhouse dorms to private rooms and even self-catering lodges. The restaurant and bar has a wide range of Scottish beers and whiskies, and serves up warming traditional foods in a lively atmosphere of live music and an open fireplace. ///daring.than.revealing

ACHNESS HOTEL, Rosehall

Nestled deep in the highlands of Sutherland, the Achness Hotel is a small hotel not far from the town of Lairg. This quiet and relaxing escape is a highly popular retreat for those looking to enjoy the local fishing, hiking, or just a weekend away from big city life.

With a total of nine rooms, all complete with a TV and bathrooms, this hotel provides all of the basics you will need for an enjoyable trip to the highlands. The onsite bar and restaurant serve up delicious food and refreshing drinks, meaning you can relax in the hotel after a long day of exploring without needing to worry about heading out. Top this all off with the traditional highland welcome that you will experience and it is no wonder this hotel is so popular in this region of Scotland. ///synthetic.looks.comedy

The Pier, Lairg

LAIRG HIGHLAND HOTEL, Lairg

Originally known as the "Nip Inn", the Lairg Highland Hotel has been serving locals and visitors for the last 20 years. Located at the southern end of Loch Shin, Lairg Highland Hotel sits just along the road from the tranquil waters of the Lairg Dam and the famous "Wee Hoose" of Lairg.

Despite its remote setting, this small highland town is alive with incredible sights and fascinating historical tales, such as the Ord Archaeology Trail, the Ord Hill Viewpoint, and, of course, the many culinary stops along the water's edge such as the Pier cafe.

Inside the hotel itself, guests can enjoy a cooked Scottish breakfast each morning and the Thistle Lounge and Bistro are open to the public for lunch and dinner.
///motivates.holly.hairspray

LOCH SHIN LUXURY PODS, Lairg

Close to the tranquil shores of the long body of water known as Loch Shin, this small collection of glamping pods offers a peaceful retreat to the mountains with stunning views of the southern highlands. Each of the four luxury pods are equipped with all of the basic necessities that you will need for a comfortable and enjoyable stay, combining the tranquility of camping with the luxury of fixed walls and a comfortable bed.

In addition to the four self-catering pods, the site at Loch Shin Luxury Pods also contains a communal area with a large field to stretch your legs and play games in, as well as a communal fire pit for socialising after a long day of adventure.
///rucksack.tidal.timing

THE PIER, Lairg

Located in Lairg, just a short drive inland from the coast, The Pier cafe has one of the most scenic views on the North Coast 500. This small and intimate cafe has a huge range of delicious and warming meals, from homemade soups to locally sourced and freshly caught fish.

The owners Gregor and Catrina also provide a mouthwatering selection of cakes that will sit well with a tea or coffee as you soak up the stunning view over Loch Shin. The interior design of the cafe/restaurant directly reflects the view outside, as the walls are tastefully decorated with refreshingly bright and airy colours and nautical-themed items to suit the strong angling heritage that Lairg has.

The menus at The Pier are also very friendly to those with specific dietary requirements, with a wide range of vegan and vegetarian options. The staff are also happy to help with any other specific dietary requirements and aim to adapt any meal to suit your needs.
///merit.clustered.cracking

PONDSIDE CAMPING, Lairg
Set upon three acres of grassland, high up on the banks of Loch Shin, the Pondside Camping grounds offer a peaceful place to pitch up and enjoy the beauty of the Sutherland wilderness. The site features grass pitches for tents and vehicles, static caravan hire, "tin tents" for rental, and a self-catering apartment for those looking for something a little more luxurious.

Amenities onsite include a block with showers and toilets; an outdoors, covered kitchen area for washing up and preparing food; and a social area for everyone to come together to enjoy.
///permanent.amps.spending

LAIRG GLAMPING PODS, Torroble
If you are looking for a peaceful getaway in the Scottish Highlands, then Lairg Glamping Pods is the place for you. The pods here are referred to as snugs, which reflects how cosy and comfortable they are to stay in, with magnificent views across the Scottish Highlands.

EAT
££

STAY
££

NC5⊕○

The 'wee hoose' on the loch, Lairg

You might be lucky to see some wild animals around the croft during your stay. Make sure to look out for red squirrels, deer, woodpeckers and other birds including rarely spotted red kites.
///landmark.dice.duties

GRANNIE'S HEILAN' HAME, Embo
The perfect beachfront location for a break, whether you stay in one of their rental lodges or caravans or on the touring area of the site. Embo beach is only a short walk away from the holiday park and is one of the most beautiful beaches in the area.

At Grannie's Heilan' Hame you can expect plenty of entertainment as there is an indoor swimming pool, a tennis court and a mini golf course. As well as a restaurant and coffee shop on site, there is also a fish and chips takeaway.
///director.lightens.unite

BIRDWATCHER'S CABIN, Golspie
Hidden away deep in the Loch Fleet Nature Reserve is the tranquil retreat known as the Birdwatcher's Cabin. This magical escape from the hustle of modern day life offers a peaceful place to relax with stunning, panoramic views of Loch Fleet and the mountains of Easter Ross to the west.

The cabin itself consists of a one bedroom, self-catering accommodation, featuring a large studio area containing the kitchen, living area and bedroom. The front face of the cabin is made up of two large, floor-to-ceiling windows, offering spectacular views of Loch Fleet. There is also an external balcony at the front, which is the perfect place to enjoy the tranquility of the surrounding area, as well as to try to spot the local wildlife of the Balblair Woods, such as pine martens, squirrels and ospreys.
///lightbulb.explorer.organ

EAT &
STAY
£

STAY
£££

NC5❀❀

CAMPING@GOLSPIE, Golspie

A newly developed campsite in the village of Golspie, this camping area is perfectly located near to the local bars and restaurants, an is just a short walk to the seaside. Right on the A9, this campsite has a total of 18 pitches, 16 of which offer electrical hookup. It also has onsite facilities for waste disposal, fresh water collection, and has an accessible toilet for communal use.

This campsite is hugely popular for those touring the NC500 route with an interest in making the most of Golspie's huge range of outdoor activities, from hiking to mountain biking. Other nearby sights include the peaceful walk to Big Burn Falls and the splendour of the ancient Dunrobin Castle.
///debt.magically.firmer

COFFEE BOTHY, Golspie

A small and cosy coffee shop in the heart of the village of Golspie, the Coffee Bothy makes use of an old, traditional bothy building, with its low roof and quaint charm. This small cafe serves up delicious homemade foods, from cakes to sandwiches and soups, and is very popular with the locals. Open all morning and afternoon, this is the perfect place to stop off for a hot breakfast on your way north through Sutherland.
///blunders.canine.ambushes

Dunrobin Cottage, Golspie

STAY
£££

NC500

DUNROBIN COTTAGES, Golspie

A number of properties dotted around the Dornoch of region Easter Ross, all in close proximity to the beautiful sights of Dunrobin Castle, Big Burn Falls, and the towering presence of the Duke of Sutherland Statue. The six luxury cottages known as the Dunrobin Cottages each offer their own style of tranquility and relaxation, from the peaceful banks of Loch Fleet to isolated escape of the Keeper's Cottage.

This collection of cottages is designed to offer a relaxing escape to the highlands of Scotland to explore the underappreciated area of Sutherland.
///waltz.makeovers.thinnest

EAT &
STAY
££

GOLSPIE INN HOTEL, Golspie

A relaxed and welcoming hotel and restaurant, situated just one mile from the magical Dunrobin Castle, the Golspie Inn Hotel is a popular spot for a delicious meal and a comfortable place to spend the night.

This inn dates back as far as 1808, when it was once known as the Sutherland Arms. Since then it has gone through multiple extensions and refurbishments and now consists of a bright dining conservatory, a cosy lounge bar with a wide range of drinks, and a beautiful garden area to enjoy on a summers day.
///fortnight.emulating.retina

EAT
£

POPPY'S COFFEE SHOP, Golspie

A delicious take-away or sit-in experience in the village of Golspie, Poppy's Coffee Shop serves a variety of home-cooked meals and cakes, baked with love. Poppy's offers hot breakfasts and lunches for those passing through Golspie and provides the perfect opportunity to stop off in this beautiful village and explore the charms it has to offer.
///verve.branded.caskets

THE WEE PINK SHOP CAPALDI'S OF BRORA, Golspie

EAT
£

The unmistakable exterior of the Capaldi's "Wee Pink Shop" sits on the High Street of Brora, unmistakable partly because of the giant novelty ice-cream cone that decorates the doorway, but mostly due to its colourful decor. Nestled amongst the old, grey buildings that line the main street of Brora, Capaldi's bright pink facade is a welcome sight in the summer months when an ice-cream by the sea is all you really want.

Capaldi's has been serving up homemade ice-cream here in Brora for over 60 years, originally from this very shop and, for a while, from a similar shop along the street. One thing that has remained the same over the decades, however, is the popularity of the delicious, fresh, sweet treats they have to offer.
///plausible.factories.scramble

BRORA CARAVAN CLUB SITE, Brora

STAY
£

Overlooking the stunning sands of Brora Beach, the Brora Caravan Club Site is a beautiful campsite sitting just outside of the cute village of Brora. Just 300 yards from the seaside, this campsite is the perfect place to escape the modern world and lose yourself in the tranquility of the Scottish highlands. It is also the perfect place to go wildlife spotting along the shore, with frequent sightings of dolphins, porpoises, seals and plenty of birds.

The campsite itself consists of a total of 54 pitches for touring vehicles and four pitches for tents. There is also a toilet block with showers, as well as laundry and dishwashing facilities.
///study.skid.safety

CLYNELISH FARM B&B, Brora

STAY
£

NC500

What better place could there be to rest your head in the Scottish highlands than in a traditional B&B just down the road from a famous whisky distillery? Built in 1865, the Clynelish Farm B&B was originally constructed for the Sutherland Estates, however, it is now used to greet guests to the highlands as a beautiful and welcoming home from home.

The Clynelish Whisky Distillery, Brora

The B&B consists of four bedrooms available to rent, all beautifully decorated and fitted with the little touches to make your stay one to remember. There is also a separate two-bedroom annex, known as the "servants quarter" that can be rented by a party for private use. All of this less than two hundreds metres from the fantastic Clynelish Distillery. What a dream location!
///stuffing.templates.fiery

COCOA SKYE, Brora
Cocoa Skye is a brilliant cafe and restaurant in the area of Brora in South East Sutherland, owned by mother and daughter Wendy and Cara. At Cocoa Skye you can indulge in some delicious food, such as made to order Belgian waffles or a luxury hot chocolate. The menu also includes savoury options, such as soup and toasties, all just a short walk from the beautiful Brora Sands beach.
///funky.spot.majors

EAT
£

NC500 PODS, Brora
The NC500 Pods are located just outside the village of Brora and offer scenic views across the countryside. There are a number of small pods containing a bed, bathroom and cooking facilities, not to mention the comfortable pull-out couch in the living room area. One of the pods is a larger honeymoon suite with floor-to-roof length windows showing off the views from the bed.

Outside the pods is a wooden barrel sauna that can be enjoyed after a day of exploring. The sauna also has a window overlooking the greenery outside.
///trickled.grins.viewer

STAY
£££

ROYAL MARINE HOTEL, Brora
This 20th century manor house overlooks the world-famous Brora Golf Course and has stunning views of the open ocean beyond. In addition to the hotel's beautifully decorated rooms, there is also an onsite restaurant, the Curing Yard, which offers a wide selection of locally sourced and inspired Scottish meals.

EAT &
STAY
£££

As well as the local attractions, such as Brora Beach and Dunrobin Castle, this hotel also offers a range of guided tours such as local walking tours, guided bike tours or Scottish Highland Tours to explore the sights further afield. For those looking to relax there is an onsite spa, known as the Bliss Spa, where you can enjoy a range of treatments in the luxurious setting of the Royal Marine Hotel.
///pushover.seats.shade

SID'S SPICE, Brora

In the heart of the quiet village of Brora sits one of the best Indian restaurants in the UK, Sid's Spice Restaurant and Takeaway. Voted the top Indian restaurant in Scotland by the Herald newspaper, Sid's Spice brings the authentic flavours of Bangladesh to the highlands of Scotland.

Whether you want a big night out or a quiet night in, Sid's Spice offers both a dine-in experiences and curry-to-go. The restaurant itself is BYO so you can bring your own drink of choice with no charge for corkage. We highly recommend the Tikka Masala as it was one of the best we have ever had.
///marathons.arming.tumblers

BANNOCKBURN INN, Helmsdale

This small, traditional and family friendly inn sits in the heart of the small fishing village of Helmsdale on the eastern coast of the Scottish Highlands. This small and cosy inn proudly serves the same purpose that similar inns have done throughout the centuries, offering a welcoming watering hole for weary travellers in search of food and drink, as well as a place to rest their heads for the night.

The Bannockburn Inn consists of a restaurant and bar area, which serves the traditional Scottish grub that you will find across most of the highlands, as well as a number of comfortable rooms to spend the night in for a very reasonable price. Given its central location along the eastern coastline, this is a popular stop off point for those travelling north to John o' Groats.
///dumplings.garden.unrated

The harbour at Helmsdale

BELGRAVE ARMS, Helmsdale

Built in 1819, this small, family run hotel was once used during the Second World War as an Officers' Mess room for military personnel stationed in the nearby area. A safe haven for friends to meet up, share a meal and discuss the "goings-on" in the local area, this reputation continues to this day as the home for good food and warm hospitality.

The rooms in the hotel feature a mixture of en-suite and shared bathroom facilities, as well as tea and coffee making facilities, and TVs. It is also just a short walk down to the seafront of Helmsdale harbour where you can enjoy the beautiful views of the open ocean.
///unwind.clips.recording

HELMSDALE LODGE HOSTEL, Helmsdale

A comfortable accommodation popular with those exploring the NC500 or travelling from Land's End to John o' Groats. There are six en-suite bedrooms that sleep up to four people. Located in the scenic village of Helmsdale, this hostel is conveniently located on the cycling and walking routes and is only a short walk from the restaurants and shops in the town.

Formerly an old gymnasium built in 1931, this building has been restored over the years to maintain its originality. The high ceilings create a bright and spacious area, perfect for the open-plan dining and lounge area and the fully equipped self-catering kitchen.
///bake.bearable.tips

TIMESPAN HERITAGE AND ARTS CENTRE CAFE, Helmsdale

Inside the Timespan Heritage and Arts Centre sits a cafe with a stunning view over the River Helmsdale. Using locally grown vegetables to produce sustainable and delicious, homecooked foods, the team at the Timespan cafe work hard to create a wide range of lunches, as well as cakes and hot drinks.
///unwind.musically.footpath

THYME AND PLAICE, Helmsdale

This coffee house and restaurant serves up locally grown foods and freshly caught seafood to create a delicious and inclusive menu for breakfast and lunch. The ever-changing menu at Thyme and Plaice uses the freshest ingredients that are readily available in the surrounding regions to produce a menu that also has a good number of imaginative vegetarian and vegan options. The team at Thyme and Plaice is also very welcoming to those with other specific dietary requirements.
///prawn.extremely.trouser

EAT
£

THE OLD SCHOOL HOUSE, Wick

The Old School House is a new self-catering accommodation overlooking the stunning stretch of sand that is Strathy Beach. This secluded two-story house offers guests a home away from home with all the facilities you could need, including a very comfortable bed to get into after a day of exploring.

The Old School House is in close proximity to many of the beautiful beaches along the north coast, including a short drive to Strathy. This comfortable home will provide you with a relaxing stay on your trip to Scotland's north coast.
///passages.crowd.overpower

STAY
£££

FORSS HOUSE HOTEL, Forss

Forss House Hotel is a magnificent hotel to base yourself at during your adventure along the north coast of Scotland. The external features resemble an old manor building and the hotel sits beside a peaceful flowing river – ideal for a relaxing walk during your stay.

The bedrooms are beautifully furnished featuring distinctly Scottish interior that create a relaxing environment. The restaurant at Forss House is the only restaurant in Caithness that has two rosettes and is regarded as one of the finest dining establishments in the north. The bar area stocks over 300 whiskies ready for you to taste.
///newer.catching.unveils

EAT &
STAY
££

NC5◉○

Melvich Hotel, Melvich

HALLADALE INN AND NORTH COAST TOURING PARK, Melvich

Just a short walk from the stunning stretch of sand that is Melvich Beach is the Halladale Inn and Touring Park. This campsite welcomes all types of touring vehicles and tents, and also has six glamping pods that can be rented for those looking for a bit more luxury. There is also a full amenities block with showers and toilets, and a licensed cafe onsite that provides cooked meals for breakfast, lunch, and dinner for guests.

///scripted.bubble.toolbar

SALMON LANDINGS, Strathy

The Strathy Point peninsula stretches far out into the North Atlantic, with stunning views of the entire coastline of the UK to the south and the open ocean to the north. Nestled amongst the rolling hills on this peninsula is the 4-star guest house known as the Salmon Landings. Originally purposed as an old salmon fishing station in 1902, Salmon Landings now welcomes guests to enjoy the breathtaking views from the high cliffs of the northern coast.

The guesthouse has four king-sized rooms on offer, all with an en-suite bathroom, as well as complimentary tea and coffee making facilities in each room. The hosts also offer a cooked breakfast for guests to enjoy before starting the day and can also, on request, provide a packed lunch to take with you on a day of adventures.

///layover.paddocks.cyber

STAY
£££

STRATHY BAY PODS, Strathy

A set of luxury glamping pods sitting above one of the most beautiful beaches in Sutherland, the Stathy Bay Pods take the term "glamping" to new heights. The interior decor of these pods instantly makes you feel at home, with their plush cushions, white panelled walls, and large, comfortable beds. It really is no wonder these pods are held in such high regard.

Each of the three pods at Strathy Bay has its own unique design, with two featuring a king-sized bed and pull-out couch, and one with two sets of bunk beds. All three enjoy unspoilt views over the golden sands of Strathy Beach and the open ocean, all right from bed.
///entitles.grief.whistle

EAT &
STAY
£

STRATHY INN, Strathy

For 200 years, the Strathy Inn has stood resolute on the northern coastline of the UK, sheltering travellers from the biting wind and rain of this remote part of the world. Today, the Strathy Inn continues this tradition by welcoming guests to the highlands of Scotland and providing a comfortable place to eat and stay on the North Coast 500 road trip.

Owners, Craig and Heather, are proud to welcome visitors to Scotland to this old coaching inn, whether it is to stay the night or simply to enjoy a meal in the restaurant and bar. The restaurant serves up home-cooked foods that contain fresh and locally sourced ingredients wherever possible. The top recommendation for the Strathy Inn is to try the local speciality: chocolate haggis. Don't knock it till you've tried it!
///trifling.support.nature

The Store Cafe, Bettyhill

ARMADALE HOUSE, Armadale
Built in 1854, this Victorian Manor House sits on the northern coast of Sutherland and now acts as a B&B for visitors to the region. It is currently still going through restoration to return the manor to the beauty and elegance that it had over one hundred years ago, however, in the meantime, guests can still enjoy the comfort and luxury that this old manor house has to offer.

The Bed and Breakfast has three guest bedrooms, aptly named the Yellow, Red, and Blue rooms after the colour schemes inside. One of the bedrooms features an en-suite bathroom and all bedrooms have access to the shared kitchen facilities, with the option to prepare your own food or request that a meal be prepared for you.
///cuddling.enjoyable.city

BETTYHILL HOTEL, Bettyhill
The Bettyhill Hotel is an exquisite hotel on the northern coast of Scotland featuring the most incredible sea views across Torrisdale Bay. Dating back to 1819, this popular hotel has had a number of changes made to it over the years. It was extended in 1869 and more recently it was renovated giving the rooms and en-suite bathrooms a very modern feel. Many of the rooms have sea views and are very bright. Bettyhill Hotel is open to the public to enjoy a fresh meal in their charming dining area.
///earphones.dial.exhaled

FARR BAY INN, Bettyhill
In the highland village of Bettyhill sits the grand manor of the Farr Bay Inn. Overlooking the popular surf spot of Far Beach, with its golden sands and crystal clear water, this 200-year-old building now acts as a hotel for Bettyhill, with a cosy bar, onsite restaurant, and beer garden for those rare sunny days in the Scottish highlands.

In addition to the bar and restaurant, the Farr Bay Inn also has a coffee house, which sells freshly ground coffee and a range of other hot drinks.
///affirming.encrusted.sector

THE STORE CAFE, Bettyhill

EAT
£

What began as the grocery store for the region of northern Sutherland over 100 years ago continues on today as a meeting place for locals to catch up, only this time over a cup of coffee and a fresh slice of cake. The Store Cafe in Bettyhill sits high upon the hillside of this small village, not far from the stunning stretch of sand known as Farr Bay.

At the Store Cafe you can enjoy home-cooked foods and fresh coffee within the original decor of the old store house, with history literally marked on the shelves of the main room. Take a closer look at some of the wooden shelves and you will be surprised to see some of the original brand names of the items that they once stocked.
///filer.outlawing.slid

BORGIE LODGE HOTEL, Borgie

EAT &
STAY
££

Hidden far off the beaten track, the Borgie Lodge Hotel sits nestled amongst the trees and moorlands of the wilderness of Northern Sutherland. Less than a mile south of the stunning and almost inaccessible Torrisdale Bay, Borgie Lodge is the definition of a highland retreat, with nothing but nature surrounding you and with stunning views of the incredible Scottish landscape.

The hotel has a range of rooms for guests to spend the night, from double rooms, all with en-suites, to a bunkhouse with two bedrooms and six bunkbeds for larger parties. All guests can enjoy a breakfast to start the day off, and the especially early risers might even catch a glimpse of the red deer that are often spotted around the hotel at night and early morning.
///interest.keyboards.vandalism

KYLE OF TONGUE COTTAGES, Coldbackie

STAY
££

Based just north of one of the most beautiful areas in Sutherland, the Kyle of Tongue cottages are a small family run business featuring a small collection of unique, self-catering cottages. Ideal for travellers who wish to explore the northern regions

The old ice house at Torrisdale Bay

at their own pace in the comfort of their "home from home", the cottages are equipped with everything you will need for a luxurious stay in the highlands.

Each of the three cottages features incredible views of the surrounding landscape, from Coldbackie and the entrance to Tongue Bay, to the small crofting village of Melness on the northern shores of the bay.

What makes this area of Scotland so special is the ever-changing environment of the bay itself, which goes from a turquoise paradise at high tide to a golden sandy beach as the tide almost entirely retreats. Pair this with the spectacular views of the impressive remains of Castle Varrich to the southern end of the bay, as well as the striking silhouette of Ben Loyal in the distance, and the result is one of the most beautiful places in the UK.
///popping.escalates.contour

BEN LOYAL HOTEL AND GLAMPING PODS, Tongue

STAY
££

Named after one of the most striking mountains in the north of Scotland, the Ben Loyal Hotel sits in the shadow of its namesake's towering peaks. This hotel is located in the heart of the village of Tongue and is perfectly situated for the local sights and nearby pubs and restaurants.

NC500

Just a six-minute walk from the ancient ruins of Castle Varrich, the hotel boasts stunning views of Tongue Bay and the causeway that spans its breadth. In addition to the variety of rooms that the hotel offers, there is also a selection of glamping pods and a self-catering lodge. There is also an in-house restaurant serving breakfast for guests and dinner for any visitors looking for a delicious traditional meal.
///synthetic.assemble.pesky

KYLE HOUSE, Tongue

STAY
£££

At the southern tip of the Kyle of Tongue lies the boutique self-catering lodge known as Kyle House. Owned and run by WildLand, this cottage is furnished and styled with a contemporary style and Scottish comfort in mind, creating a warm and welcoming space to escape the harsh northern weather outside.

Everything about this house, from the heavy and inviting front door, to the cosy living quarters and sumptuous free-standing bathtub, reflects the ethos of the Kyle House: Stay where the world can't find you.
///scream.glance.directors

STAY
£

KYLE OF TONGUE HOSTEL AND CAMPSITE, Tongue

Views of the breathtaking, rugged landscape of the region of Tongue do not get much better than those enjoyed at the Kyle of Tongue Hostel and Campsite. Overlooking the bay at the eastern end of the Tongue causeway, this campsite has panoramic views of everything from the mouth of the bay to the inland view of Castle Varrich and the distant silhouette of Ben Loyal.

As well as space for tents and touring vehicles to park up for the night, there is also a hostel with five rooms that have access to the guest lounge and fireplace. There is also a choice of three self-catering rooms, consisting of two static caravans and one cottage.
///instance.ventures.youths

STAY
£££

LUNDIES HOUSE, Tongue

A stylish, boutique accommodation overlooking the breathtaking Bay of Tongue, Lundies House is a 17th century manse that has been restored with exquisite detail for visitors to enjoy its luxury. Decorated with a Scandinavian inspiration, the minimalist interior gently whispers luxury from every fine detail that has been put in. It is the latest property from Wildland.Scot, whose aim is to "rewild" the areas of Scotland that have experienced the harsh grip of humankind throughout the centuries.

A stay in Lundies House is more than just a visit to a guest house, with each meal delivering a sensory journey and every

The ruins of Varrich Castle, Tongue

day consisting of a new adventure. Guests will enjoy meals freshly prepared by the in-house chefs, who serve an ever-changing menu of locally sourced ingredients in a delicious and creative way. Upon request, guests can also take part in organised tours with local experts that provide an insight into the local history and landscape and also showcase the best sights that the region has to offer.

///kicks.notes.masts

EAT &
STAY
£££

NC500

TONGUE HOTEL, Tongue

Originally built in the 1800s to act as a shooting lodge in the highlands of Scotland, Tongue Hotel has since been renovated and extended over the years. The hotel sits at the top of the hill in Tongue, meaning the upper rooms can enjoy stunning views over the Bay of Tongue and ruins of Castle Varrich.

Each of the rooms at the Tongue Hotel is individually designed to reflect the periods that the hotel has lived through, with wood panelling throughout the hotel, as well as open fires and antique furniture to complete the look. The rooms are equipped with all of the expected luxuries, such as TVs, tea and coffee facilities, and even a decanter of sherry to enjoy upon your arrival.

At the main entrance of the hotel, the restaurant and bar area is open to everyone and serves up a fantastic range of local cuisine, all produced with locally sourced ingredients wherever possible, the restaurant and bar is a popular spot for visitors to Tongue for lunch and dinner.

///liner.placidly.potato

EAT
£

WEAVERS CAFE, Tongue

Weavers Cafe is a locally focussed business with sea views over Tongue. Previously the old school house, a lot of locals feel familiarity visiting Weavers Cafe and enjoying the great selection of food and drinks on offer. As well as serving a range of hot meals and cakes, catering to dietary requirements, Weavers Cafe also hosts a gift shop selling a large variety of goods, including NC500 memorabilia.

///chuckling.indoor.tastings

BAYVIEW CARAVAN AND CAMPSITE, Talmine

Bayview Caravan and Campsite is located on the shores of Talmine Bay, just off the main NC500 route. The campsite is small and the pitches have beautiful views across the bay. Electric hook-up is not currently available at Bayview Caravan and Campsite, however other facilities, such as a toilet block with showers, chemical waste disposal and fresh water are provided.

Bayview Caravan and Campsite is a great base for exploring the north coast of Scotland. There are beaches nearby as well as some hikes with fantastic views.

Melness, a short walk from Bayview Campsite, has a well-stocked shop and post office and a craft shop selling locally made goods. In the neighbouring village of Tongue you will find two hotels, both with public bars and restaurants, a shop with post office and 24/7 self-service fuel pumps.
///nails.giraffes.acre

ISLAND VIEW GLAMPING PODS, Talmine

The Island View Glamping Pods are a family run project located in Talmine, near the breathtaking Kyle of Tongue. These pods offer a comfortable stay with stunning views that overlook the clear water of Talmine Bay and the islands that sit isolated in the mouth of the Kyle. This quiet location is one of the lesser-known regions of the North Coast 500 and is a perfect spot for a relaxing vacation far removed from the crowds.
///necklace.stumpy.cassettes

View over Tongue from Castle Varrich

DURNESS YOUTH HOSTEL, Durness

STAY
£

Overlooking the cliffs of Durness, high above the entrance to the impressive Smoo Cave, are the long, tin-roof cabins of the Durness Youth Hostel. The ideal base for those looking to explore the North Coast 500 on a budget, without sacrificing home comforts of a comfortable bed and a warm shower, this hostel is a popular stop-over for visitors to the region. Guests can even enjoy a continental breakfast supplied by the hostel, or can prepare food of their own using the well-equipped kitchen facilities.

NC500

///fluffed.dried.answer

MACKAY'S ROOMS, Durness

STAY
£££

In the heart of the thriving highland town of Durness, Mackay's Rooms is a boutique B&B that sits proudly on the main street. The grey exterior of the original 18th century building couples nicely with the modern twist of the conservatory extension at the front of the accommodation, reflecting the renovation and restoration that this hotel has recently experienced.

Inside the B&B, each of the seven bedrooms is decorated to its own unique design, all finished with a level of charm and luxury that is sure to create a memorable trip. In addition to the rooms, Mackay's Rooms also offers a range of self-catering accommodations spread throughout the area of Durness. Each of these properties has their own unique quirks, making every stay at them different from the last.

///trifling.clusters.evaporate

SANGO SANDS OASIS, Durness

STAY
£

Sango Sands Oasis is one of the most popular campsites on the North Coast 500 as it sits high on the cliffs overlooking award-winning beaches. This campsite is open for tents, caravans and motorhomes and for those who don't require an electric hook-up, no booking is required and pitches are given on a first come, first served basis. There is a camper's kitchen with a breakfast bar for those staying in a tent and other facilities such as a new toilet block and laundry facilities onsite.

Nearby to the campsite is a mini supermarket and a petrol station. When you stay at Sango Sands Oasis, keep a look out to sea as you may be lucky enough to spot whales, seals or dolphins. It is recommended to book ahead to avoid disappointment for Sango Sands Oasis.
///cackling.bride.bumps

**EAT &
STAY
££**

SMOO CAVE HOTEL, Durness
Hidden from view of the land, Smoo Cave is an enormous sea cave that was once used as a safe haven for the Vikings to store their longboats. As you enter the mouth of the cave, craning your neck to see the details in the roof 50ft above your head, the sound of water echoing all around you, it is easy to feel as if you are travelling through time to those days long gone. If the entrance to the cave is not enough, it is also possible to take a tour of the internal cave system at Smoo Cave and hear all about its history from the experts who have been excavating the cave over the last decade.

Back above land, to the east of the mouth of the cave sits the small, family-run hotel known as the Smoo Cave Hotel. Overlooking the bay where the entrance to the cave is, this hotel has beautiful views of the jagged coastline to the east of Scotland's northern coast. There is also an onsite bar and restaurant serving breakfast for residents and dinner for all travellers.
///agents.comedians.simulator

The entrance to Smoo Cave at Durness

EAT
£

OZONE CAFÉ, Cape Wrath

A cafe for the hardiest of adventurers, this coffee shop is perched at the very ends of the earth, far out at the northerly tip of one of Britain's largest wilderness regions, Cape Wrath. The Ozone Cafe is set within the old structure of the Cape Wrath Lighthouse, a 20m tower that was built in 1828 to warn ships of the dangers of Cape Wrath's treacherous cliffs.

This lighthouse is open to visitors all year round, whether by foot or in the minibus that Cape Wrath offers from the Keoldale ferry, south of Durness. The owner of the cafe, John Ure, is always friendly and welcoming to travellers, greeting them with a warm meal and a hot cup of tea.
///lurching.obligated.pizzeria

EAT &
STAY
£

NC500

OLD SCHOOL RESTAURANT & ROOMS, Inshegra

Overlooking the beautiful waters of Loch Inchard, this old schoolhouse now acts as a B&B for visitors to the highlands of Cape Wrath. This bed and breakfast sits on the main route to Kinlochbervie, however, thanks to its distance from the main tourist route, the surrounding area is very peaceful.

The Old School has a range of sizes of rooms available, from singles up to superior doubles, all of which have a uniquely beautiful view to be enjoyed from their windows. The onsite restaurant serves guests a complimentary Scottish breakfast to prepare them for the day ahead, and is also open for evening meals to guests and visitors.
///closer.bulbs.albums

EAT &
STAY
£

KINLOCHBERVIE HOTEL, Kinlochbervie

On the northwestern coast of Scotland, overlooking the rugged and picturesque landscape of the southern tip of Cape Wrath, sits Kinlochbervie Hotel. This friendly and welcoming hotel boasts incredible views of the fishing harbour of Kinlochbervie and the stunning coastline of Loch Inchard.

The remote and peaceful harbour village of Kinlochbervie is a fantastic place to visit in the north of Scotland due to how beautiful the surrounding area is. Rolling hills drop into crystal clear water and the distant horizon is spotted with towering mountains from a fairytale not yet written. It is the perfect base for adventures to the remote regions of Cape Wrath, such as Oldshoremore Beach and Sandwood Bay Beach, both of which exhibit such striking beauty that any visit to them begs a vow for it to not be the last.

///song.handyman.power

THE ANCHORAGE, Scourie

A lively and welcoming bar and restaurant that sits on the site of the Scourie Caravan Park, the Anchorage serves up all of the classic Scottish pub meals, from fresh fish and chips to decadent gourmet burgers.

At the Anchorage, you can expect everything that a good highland bar should offer: good food, great drinks, and a friendly and vibrant atmosphere to celebrate the end of another day of adventures.

///bars.flamenco.hubcaps

SCOURIE CARAVAN PARK, Scourie

Scourie Caravan Park features an elevated position with incredible views out to sea. It is suitable for tents, caravans and motorhomes. A short walk along the shore and you will arrive at a small sandy beach. As well as hard to beat views, Scourie Caravan Park also has a cafe/bar onsite where you can enjoy a relaxed meal or a drink.

Handa Island is a short ferry ride away and is well worth a visit while you are staying in the area. If you enjoy bird-watching, the months of May, June and July are when you will be most likely to spot puffins on Handa Island.

The fishing board at the Scourie Hotel

Scourie village is a short walk away and has a small supermarket, hotel and restaurant, this is a great base for exploring the surrounding area.
///newsprint.cried.bank

SCOURIE HOTEL, Scourie

EAT & STAY £££

What began its life as a fortified house, built by the Mackay family in the 16th-century, Scourie Hotel has played a number of roles over the centuries that followed. After changing hands to the Duke of Sutherland, this building underwent a series of alterations before becoming a coaching inn for the highland village of Scourie, originally known as the Stafford Arms.

Since then, it changed hands to the Campbell family, who bought the property in 2015 and put to work their vast experience in hospitality and catering to create a comfortable and scenic hotel that is renowned for its welcoming hospitality.

The Scourie Hotel and Restaurant sits overlooking the tranquil waters of Scourie Bay and offers not only beds but also food and drink to those in need. Using the freshest Sutherland ingredients, the team at Scourie produce a mouthwatering selection of meals. There is also a lounge and bar serving up the best malt whiskies and a choice of real ales and local craft beers.
///grinning.leaky.taxpayers

SCOURIE LODGE, Scourie

EAT & STAY ££

Sitting high above the tranquil waters of Scourie Bay is the beautiful manor house of Scourie Lodge. Built in 1835 by the Duke of Sutherland, the house was originally meant to be for his new bride, however, she preferred to stay in their original accommodation: the grand residence of Dunrobin Castle. Today, this grand house features a walled garden and caters to guests as a Bed and Breakfast in the highlands of Scotland.
///occupiers.verbs.foggy

KYLESKU HOTEL, Kylesku

A newly renovated boutique hotel overlooking the crystal clear waters of Loch Gleann Dubh, Kylesku Hotel provides the perfect accommodation to admire the beauty of the surrounding landscape. The eleven beautiful bedrooms at the Kylesku Hotel all showcase the incredible loch and mountain views of the region, as does the downstairs restaurant, which has also been named the best Informal Restaurant of the Year by the Scottish Hotel awards (twice!).

The staff at the Kylesku Hotel are proud to welcome visitors to the highlands and through the doors to enjoy the service of the hotel and restaurant. With the bountiful Loch Gleann Dubh and the surrounding crofts of Sutherland right on its doorstep, the Kylesku aims to source its seafood, meat and vegetables as locally as possible. This, in turn, guarantees the freshness of the food that makes it onto every plate in the restaurant.
///lunge.work.emerald

KYLESKU LODGES, Kylesku

Facing west along Loch a' Chàirn Bhàin, the Kylesku Lodges have incredible sunset views over the mountains of Assynt as they sit nestled amongst some of Scotland's most rugged landscape.

Each of the lodges have the use of their own private balcony to admire the beauty of the surrounding hills and deep lochs, and as if that wasn't enough, they also have their own wood-burning stoves to keep the cold at bay. They also come equipped with all of the modern home comforts that you will need, such as WIFI and a television with access to apps for streaming and watching your favourite programmes.
///commended.orbited.shipyards

134

A seafood platter at the Kylesku Hotel

NEWTON LODGE, Kylesku

Just south of the iconic sight of the Kylesku Bridge, Newton Lodge is a luxury hotel with incredibly scenic views. Each of the bedrooms at the lodge have their own unique character and style, making each return visit to this highland escape different to the last.

The hotel features a bar and restaurant that is open to the public, serving an exciting range of traditional-inspired meals, with ingredients all sourced from local suppliers. The bar has a wide range of whiskies, beers, wines and cocktails, so feel free to settle in the for night with a dram of your choice and a view to remember.
///declares.married.difficult

WEST COAST HIDEAWAYS, Nedd

This set of luxury, self-catering shepherd's huts sit nestled high up on the hills that overlook the small inlet of Loch Nedd. As with any tiny home retreat, these lodges offer a cute and quaint escape from normality, however, this time in one of the world's most spectacular environments. Each of the lodges come with its own private decking and a Swedish-style wood-burning hot tub to soak in and admire the beauty of the surrounding landscape.
///staining.issue.hopes

DRUMBEG HOTEL, Drumbeg

As the road south winds its way through Sutherland's dramatic and ever-changing landscape, the village of Drumbeg is a welcome respite to stop and admire the incredible views all around. The Drumbeg Hotel provides this rest for weary travellers as inside its welcoming, whitewash exterior lies a cosy bar, some tasty food, and a warm and comfortable bed for the night.

The Drumbeg Hotel has a total of six bedrooms, all with en-suite facilities and all uniquely decorated to suit the beauty of the surrounding landscape. The restaurant enjoys open views of the small lochan that sits opposite the town, as well as the rolling

landscape beyond, and the onsite bar is well-stocked and ready to host both residents and non-residents for a night in the wilderness.
///remainder.weddings.pebble

STOER HEAD LIGHTHOUSE, Raffin

STAY
£££

Perched on the most westerly point of Sutherland is the 14 metre-tall structure of Stoer Head Lighthouse. Built in 1870, this lighthouse has guarded the coastline for over a century. At this remote location there were once two lightkeepers, one Principal Lighthouse Keeper and one Assistant, who looked after its function until it was fully automated in 1978 and their help was no longer required.

The keeper's house remains in this location to this day, however, it now acts as two self-catering apartments for visitors who want to sleep at the edge of the world. Fully furnished with everything you need for a comfortable stay, these apartments are the best way to experience sleeping far out in the Scottish wilderness.
///care.molars.demotion

ROCK STOP CAFE AND EXHIBITION CENTRE, Unapool

EAT
£

In the heart of Scotland's most scenic region, nestled neatly on the shores of Loch Gleann Dubh is the Rock Stop Cafe and Exhibition Centre. Right here in this vast region of Sutherland, you will be able to discover some of the most fascinating geological phenomena known to mankind. The very mountains around this area have a story to tell: from tectonic shifts that happened millions of years ago, to the carving of the landscape by glaciers during the ice age.

The Rock Stop Visitor Centre is a fantastic place to learn the wonders of the natural world and how vast geological forces have created the stunning landscape that we see today. There is, of course, also the cafe, where you can relax and unwind with the spectacular view of the highlands of Scotland before you enjoy a well-earned cup of coffee and a slice of cake.

Stoer Head Lighthouse, Raffin

They also offer a selection of prepared lunches, such as sandwiches and wraps, as well as hot soup for the more traditional Scottish weather.
///dandelions.clashing.friday

INCHNADAMPH EXPLORER'S LODGE, Inchnadamph

At the foot of Ben More in the mountainous region of Assynt is the collection of budget accommodations of the Inchnadamph Explorer's Lodge. Guests have a choice of private rooms, hostel dorms, self-catering suites, shepherd's huts, or a full cottage for larger parties.

This accommodation has something for everyone and is perfectly placed for those looking to do some munro bagging or explore the nearby sights such as the haunted Ardvreck Castle or the breathtaking Wailing Widow Falls.
///whirlwind.carpets.slurs

THE INCHNADAMPH HOTEL, Inchnadamph

At the eastern point of Loch Assynt, surrounded by the towering peaks of the Assynt mountain range, is the old coaching inn that was built to host weary travellers in the region over two hundred years ago. Today, the Inchnadamph Hotel welcomes weary travellers passing through the highlands of Sutherland with a comfortable bed, a warm, home-cooked meal, and a drink with a view.

The Inchnadamph Hotel sits well back from the main road, giving it a sense of peace and solitude in this wonderful part of the world. Gazing out from the hotel at the snow-capped peaks and deep Scottish loch, it is easy to feel that sense of belonging that brings visitors back to Scotland again and again.
///stews.expert.craftsmen

CLACHTOLL BEACH CAMPSITE, Clachtoll

Five miles north of Lochinver in North West Sutherland is the stunning Clachtoll Beach. The golden sands are surrounded by sand dunes and there are wooden walkways leading down to the shore. Clachtoll Beach Campsite has magnificent views out to sea, and there is a range of facilities including serviced and unserviced pitches, toilets and showers, and a shop selling essentials.

Look out for orcas, minke whales and dolphins as they frequently visit the area. It is likely you will also see a vast range of birds such as buzzards, oystercatchers and maybe even a short-eared owl.
///defaults.issued.crazy

THE LITTLE ABODES, Clachtoll

The Little Abodes are modern glamping pods, each with their own private hot tub. A decking area sits outside the pods with beautiful panoramic sea views. Each pod sleeps two adults and two children and has a comfortable lounge area with a TV. The kitchen area features a mini-fridge, microwave, toaster and kettle to allow you to cook basic meals whilst you are staying at The Little Abodes.

The surrounding area of the north-west Scottish highlands has many great walks in the most beautiful scenery.
///hissing.cube.obliging

ACHMELVICH SHORE CAMPSITE, Achmelvich

The Achmelvich Shore Campsite has magnificent sea views and sits on the shores of Achmelvich Beach, a stunning white sand beach. There are many great walks in the area as well as Europe's smallest castle, Hermit's Castle.

There are a range of facilities on the site, including electric hook ups, laundry facilities and washing-up areas. There are hot showers in the toilet and an accessible toilet is also available.

If you need anything during your stay, there is an on-site shop and a great Fish & Chip Shop too.
///barefoot.treetop.partied

Hermit's Castle, Achmelvich

STAY
£££

NC5○○

NC500 PODS, Achmelvich

The Achmelvich NC500 Pods are a great place to stay if you are looking for a close beach location away from the town. At only a short five minute walk from one of Scotland's most beautiful beaches, Achmelvich Beach.

The pods have a comfortable double bed and lounge area with a pull out sofa, with a feature to remotely control the lights. There is a small kitchen area with an oven and a microwave.

The communal area outside hosts a seating area and a firepit, surrounded by fairylights for a peaceful summer evening.
///albums.daunted.decide

STAY
££

NC5○○

CAISTEAL LIATH CHALETS, Baddidarach

Across the water from the thriving highland village of Lochinver is the collection of self-catering chalets of Caisteal Liath. This region of Sutherland is an ideal location for wildlife spotting, isolated and unspoiled by humans, and it is very common to spot animals such as red deer and sea eagles right from your accommodation.

Each of the chalets is equipped for a luxurious stay, with a large television, sound system, full kitchen facilities, coffee machine, and a very comfortable bed. There is also a private balcony to admire the stunning views of Loch Inver, and some even have a private hot tub to relax in.
///canyons.ranked.devoured

EAT &
STAY
£

AN CALA CAFE AND BUNKHOUSE, Lochinver

At the very tip of the tranquil bay of Loch Inver sits the small harbour village of Lochinver itself. Sheltered from the storms and swells of the North Atlantic Ocean, the bay of Lochinver has been a safe refuge for boats for hundreds of years. Overlooking the bay, where the waters from Loch Culag meet the sea, is the cafe and accommodation setting known as the An Cala Cafe and Bunkhouse.

This cafe and hostel has 14 bunkbeds set over three rooms for weary travellers to rest up for a discount price. Downstairs, there is a large, open-plan cafe that is always alive with atmosphere. Serving up a host of daily specials based on the day's catch, as well as the traditional cafe grub that you would expect, such as hot soup and toasted sandwiches, An Cala is always a popular spot with visitors and locals to meet up for a coffee and a catch up.
///homecare.foremost.disprove

THE CULAG HOTEL, Lochinver

EAT & STAY

One of Lochinver's most iconic buildings, the Culag Hotel sits beside the harbour buildings of the village; its tall towers giving it an almost castle-like prowess. Originally built as a smokehouse for locally caught herring, the building was converted to a hotel in 1890 and has been used as such ever since.

With a total of 12 rooms spread out over three floors, the Culag Hotel is an excellent base for those visiting the region who are looking to explore the surrounding countryside of Lochinver.

On the ground floor, the hotel also features a restaurant and a bar, both of which are open to non-residents. The restaurant is open for evening meals, when it serves a selection of home-cooked meals, and the bar offers a selection of over 100 single malt whiskies, as well as a number of beers and wines.
///crouching.landscape.melts

DELILAH'S, Lochinver

EAT ££

Delilah's is a quirky restaurant and bar in Lochinver with incredible views across the loch.

Previously the tourist information office, Rachel and her husband have developed this building into a social hub with a beer garden and a unique menu with a great variety of options for dietary requirements.
///sling.sunbeam.mush

Delilah's, Lochinver (top)   Deer at Lochinver (bottom)

INVERLODGE HOTEL, Lochinver

EAT & STAY £££

Hidden from view above the town of Lochinver, the Inverlodge Hotel offers the ultimate escape from society with luxurious rooms, impeccable meals, and a view that is likely to stick with you forever. This 5-star hotel sits walking distance from the quaint and lively harbour village of Lochinver: perfect for those looking for a local pub to socialise in at the end of the day.

The onsite bar and restaurant serves a select menu of the finest ingredients from the local area in an environment to suit, with floor-to-ceiling views of the bay and beyond. There is also a foyer lounge where you can relax in the comfortable chairs and enjoy an afternoon tea to recharge from a day of exploring.

Nearby sights include the stunning Achmelvich Beach, the crashing Falls of Kirkaig, and the towering Suilven mountain.
///minder.named.homing

LOCHINVER LARDER, Lochinver

EAT ££

One of the most popular food stops on the North Coast 500 is Lochinver Larder. Located on the river banks is plenty of outdoor seating to enjoy a famous award-winning pie. Lochinver Larder has won awards for the best meat pie and over the past year they have won nine awards across their pies. There are over 80 different pies available, including sweet and savoury which can now also be ordered online and delivered to your door. There are options to suit dietary requirements on the main menu and the pie menu.
///gurgled.much.cherubs

NC5○O

MOUNTVIEW, Lochinver

STAY ££

The accommodation at Mountview has incredible panoramic views over Lochinver, looking towards the Assynt mountains, Suilven and Canisp. There are two self-catering log cabins that sit right on the water, a converted croft house just behind them along with a single pod.

NC5○O

Mountview is a great base for those visiting the Lochinver area, the remote location of the accommodation allows for the opportunity to witness various wildlife such as golden eagles, seals and dolphins.

///including.branching.cultivation

PEETS, Lochinver

Located in Lochinver, Peets is a family-friendly restaurant overlooking Lochinver harbour. The co-owners, David and Angie, established Peets in 2014 and have built an excellent reputable restaurant that is popular amongst both locals and tourists visiting the area.

A popular dish for visitors is the Peet's Seafood Chowder as well as other locally caught seafood. Peets also sells its own gin at the restaurant and through their online shop in collaboration with a local distiller.

///used.stress.motored

SUIL NA MARA, Lochinver

A great base for discovering the local area of Lochinver is Suil na Mara. The self-catering pod sleeps four and has incredible views over the bay. There is a seating area that folds out into a sofa bed as well as a TV, kitchen and private bathroom.

The self-catering studio is part of the main house, however feels very private as it has its own entrance. There is a double bedroom with an en-suite bathroom and a living area with a pull-out sofa bed. For your self-catering needs you can enjoy cooking in the fully equipped kitchen.

Located only a short five minute walk from the town of Lochinver, this is a great place to stay on the NC500 route.

///squeaks.headliner.foremost

The harbour in winter, Lochinver

LAZYBED ACCOMMODATION, Inverkirkaig

Looking for a quirky retreat into the wilderness, completely removed from society and with stunning views to top if off? The two eco-style cabins by Lazybed Accommodation are the perfect place for you. Nestled among the natural habitat that sits to the south of Lochinver, these two beautifully designed, one-bedroom cabins sit overlooking the peaceful waters of Loch Kirkaig.

Designed to impeccable precision using renewable Scottish timber and insulated with sheep's wool, these cabins have been built from start to finish with the idea of minimising their impact on the beauty of the surrounding environment. Each cabin has a private balcony for the warm summer days and a log fire for those colder winter nights.
///firebird.advances.tastes

ACHENINVER HOSTEL, Achiltibuie

This highly rated, walk-in hostel on the Achiltibuie peninsula has been welcoming travellers to the highlands of Scotland for over 80 years. Consisting of four sleeping pods, all equipped with a toilet, kitchen facility, and a large, luxurious bed, the hostel sits a five minute walk from the main road and car park, so be sure to pack light!

The perk of this isolated location is the mesmerising solitude that you can enjoy here in Achiltibuie. Absolute silence, apart from the noise of the wind through the heather, the nearby crashing waves, and the odd bleating of the nearby farm animals or calls of the red deer.
///leathers.appetite.pets

SUMMER ISLES HOTEL, Achiltibuie

Sitting far out on one of Scotland's most inaccessible regions is the historic Summer Isles Hotel. Built back in 1860 to act as a fishing inn for the Cromarty Estates, this hotel sits amongst the rugged beauty of the Achiltibuie peninsula, facing west towards the collection of islands known as the Summer Isles.

The restaurant in the hotel is the perfect place to enjoy a meal after a day of exploring, with incredible views of the islands and ocean, especially as the sun sets and paints the landscape a deep gold. There is also a bar that has acted as the local watering hole for over a century, with a cosy indoor area and a large outdoor beer garden to enjoy during the long summer days.
///victor.sues.stuns

CAITHNESS

Cape Wrath

Balnakeil
Craft Village
Durness

Talmine

Coldbackie

Tongue

Armadale

Strathy

Bettyhill

Borgie

ervje

Inshegra

Kylesku

Unapool

Inchnadamph

The River Bothy, Berriedale

THE RIVER BOTHY, Berriedale

EAT
££

Formerly used as an old laundrette for the Wellbeck Estate, this cute little cottage now acts as a refreshing pit-stop for all travellers at the side of the A9. With outdoor and indoor seating, a huge selection of freshly baked cakes, and a warm and welcoming smile when you enter, the River Bothy is the perfect place to enjoy a morning coffee as you head north.

One of the River Bothy's most unique charms is how well preserved the interior of the building remains today. As you enter the building and head through to the gift shop and additional seating on the right, you can find the original boiler, drying racks, and heat vents that were once used to wash and dry the clothes. Take a trip through Scottish history, all while you enjoy a fresh cup of coffee at the River Bothy.
///swordfish.uniforms.warned

THE BAY DUNBEATH, Dunbeath

EAT &
STAY
££

One of Caithness' hidden gems, the small harbour village of Dunbeath is a quiet haven with stunning views of the cliffs and Dunbeath Castle to the south. Recently renovated, the Bay Dunbeath offers a welcome shelter and warming grub for travellers making their way north or south along the A9.

With a wide range of pub food on offer, including wood-fired, gourmet pizza options, The Bay is a perfect spot to stop off for a bite to eat and a stroll along the beautiful, stony beach of Dunbeath.
///knowledge.crouches.invent

DUNBEATH COASTAL RETREAT, Dunbeath

STAY
££

Dunbeath Coastal Retreat has recently opened up alongside The Bay Dunbeath and currently features four beautiful eco cabins. Only a short walk from the beach, guests are welcomed to come and enjoy a relaxing stay in this area of naturally beauty. The cabins feature high quality furnishings, a shower room and toilet with toiletries and plush towels supplied. There is also a kitchenette and breakfast baskets can be delivered to your door.
///knowledge.crouches.invent

TASTY TOES – SHELLFISH TO GO, Dunbeath

Situated just 200 metres from the harbour, you will not find seafood much fresher than that at Tasty Toes in Dunbeath. This small pop-up van can be found next to the harbour parking area and sells a selection of shellfish, all freshly caught and locally prepared by the owners.

If you are looking for a friendly face and a unique bite to eat then Tasty Toes is the place to go!
///chicken.unleashed.chuck

FORSE OF NATURE, Latheron

Enjoy an escape to the countryside with a beautifully tranquil stay at the Forse of Nature Guest House. This bespoke, family run accommodation is entirely unique to the highlands of Scotland, with a sole focus on working with nature to live a "simple, sustainable, and affordable" way of life.

Set in the grand building of Forse House, this restored care home works to protect and promote the beauty of nature in the region, with locally sourced fresh foods, upcycled and eco-friendly furniture and decorations, and growing investments into renewable energy to reduce the accommodation's carbon footprint.

The Forse of Nature guest house is aimed at those seeking a simple, quiet, and affordable setting to enjoy their time in the peaceful east highlands of Scotland. Each room is tastefully decorated with a unique style, and rooms are sized to be able to suit most groups of friends and families. It is a setting far removed from modern civilisation and is perfect for those looking to spend time amongst nature and away from the modern-day rat race.
///lung.conductor.denser

BAYVIEW HOTEL, Lybster

Overlooking the small and tranquil harbour of the village of Lybster, the Bayview Hotel is a small, family run hotel with a selection of room sizes, varying from single rooms to family

Forse of Nature, Latheron

sized rooms. There is also an onsite restaurant and bar that is popular with those looking for a cosy and welcoming atmosphere, an open fire on a cold day, and a range of activities, from pool tournaments to pub quizzes.

Comfortable, reliable and basic, the Bayview Hotel is a great stopping point halfway along Caithness' beautiful eastern coastline.
///headache.slide.paler

NORTH STAR GLAMPING, Lybster

North Star Glamping is conveniently located on the North Coast 500 route in Lybster, a short drive from John o' Groats in the Caithness region. Both luxury pods have a double bed and come with the option to sleep an additional two people on the pull-out settee. This self-catering accommodation features a small kitchen with amenities for cooking and eating and there is an outdoor picnic area to eat out at when the weather is in your favour. There is also a communal firepit on site that you can enjoy with kindling and firelighters provided.
///specifies.samples.sunroof

THE PORTLAND HOTEL, Lybster

The Portland Hotel can be found in the quiet village of Lybster in Caithness. It was made famous during the popular Netflix show "The Crown" as it was used as the make-up and costume change base for the cast whilst they were filming in the area.

The hotel features 22 unique en-suite rooms with a range of bedroom sizes and a cold buffet and Scottish breakfast is included. A great selection of food is served up in the restaurant throughout the day with a range of options to suit different dietary requirements.
///warned.regard.elsewhere

THRUMSTER HOUSE, Thrumster

STAY
£

Set within 20 acres of green woodlands and tranquil gardens is the welcoming family home of Thrumster House. For years, this B&B has been providing a highland welcome to guests in the region of Caithness, with two bedrooms consisting of a twin room and a double room.

The house is also perfectly situated near to the village of Thrumster, with the local pub within walking distance and local sights such as the Castle of Old Wick, the Whaligoe Steps, and the many archaeological sites of Caithness.
///surpassed.isolating.books

PULDAGON FARM SHOP AND RESTAURANT, Puldagon

EAT
££

A family owned business since the early 20th century, the Puldagon Farm has recently expanded its custom from purely farming to offer visitors the finest quality produce and freshly prepared meals in the shop and cafe. The Puldagon Farm is situated just three miles from the northern town of Wick and has been serving happy customers food and drink since 2019.

Serving up breakfast, lunch, and dinner options, as well as a host of locally sourced produce in the farm shop section, the Puldagon Farm Shop and Restaurant is a fantastic place to stop-off and stock-up in Caithness before you continue on your way along the coast.
///named.flaked.lentil

DEVITA'S PIZZERIA AND CAFE, Wick

EAT
££

Devita's Pizzeria and Cafe is one of the best pizzerias in the area and is popular for both dining in and take-away food. The pizzeria is family run and aims to bring you a taste of Italy from the province of Brindisi, where Devita's originates from. The staff are very friendly and welcome you into the pizzeria to relax in the atmosphere and enjoy their delicious food.
///flask.unveils.waltz

Printers Rest, Wick

MACKAYS HOTEL, Wick

Fancy a bite to eat on the shortest street in the world? Then Mackays Hotel is the place for you. This award-winning and family run hotel offers a warm and welcoming bed for the night with a choice of 30 en-suite rooms, ranging in size from singles to family sized rooms.

If you are looking to sample some of Scotland's finest Single Malt Whisky or are just looking to relax with a cocktail of your choice then the Mackays Bar is the perfect place to do so. So much so that the proud owner of Mackays Hotel actually holds a merit qualification from the Scotch Whisky Association, so you can relax knowing you are in good hands.

For lunch and evening meals, the onsite restaurant, No. 1 Bistro, offers a range of freshly prepared meals using locally sourced ingredients.
///originals.resorting.weeds

MORAGS, Wick

Morags is a great cafe in the town centre of Wick serving a variety of hot food and cakes. There are plenty of seats both inside and outside as well as a children's 'pirate-themed' play area.
///when.defected.according

NETHERCLIFFE HOTEL, Wick

The Nethercliffe Hotel is one of the oldest buildings in the country, created from a dwelling that was built in 1824 during the time of an extension to the existing fishing harbour. At this time, Wick, where the hotel is situated, was growing to be one of the busiest herring fishing ports in the world. There are six fairly sized en-suite bedrooms and a south-facing garden for guests to enjoy. It is only a short walk into the town centre of Wick from the Nethercliffe Hotel.

The restaurant serves delicious food and all dietary requirements can be catered for.
///wreck.avocado.dean

EAT &
STAY
££

NC500

EAT
£

EAT &
STAY

PRINTERS REST, Wick

The former site of the old John o' Groats printing building, the Printers Rest is now home to one of the top 50 restaurants in Scotland. This small restaurant, run by the lovely Karen and John, brings a Maltese fusion to a traditional Scottish menu, using the Mediterranean foods that Karen enjoyed in Malta as inspiration.

In addition to offering freshly cooked and prepared cafe and deli foods, with a wide range of vegetarian and vegan options, the Printers Rest also contains a wool shop and sells a range of local crafts for those in search of souvenirs.

The Printers Rest ethos involves small batch cooking to reduce food waste and ensure all food is prepared as freshly as possible. This means that no matter when you visit this intimate restaurant, you will always be offered the best produce that could be sourced at that time, resulting in an ever changing menu prepared with love.
///nametag.smirks.darling

WICKERS WORLD, Wick

Overlooking the historical harbour of Wick, the Wickers World has been proudly serving food and drink to locals and visitors alike for years. One of the unique features of this cafe is the view that you can enjoy with your meal, featuring the busy harbour and the boats that frequent it on a daily basis, from large container ships to small fishing boats.

Wickers World also doubles as a cosy B&B with four en-suite rooms suitable for everyone from solo travellers to families. Any visit to this local cafe and B&B is a welcome one with owners Vic and Val ready to help all visitors as best they can to enjoy their trip around the Scottish Highlands.
///operating.depending.noisy

Noss Head Lighthouse, Noss Head

STAY
£££

NOSS HEAD LIGHTHOUSE, Noss Head

Perched at the very end of the Noss Head peninsula, overlooking the beautiful stretch of coastline to the north known as Sinclair's Bay is the Noss Head Lighthouse. This 18 metre high lighthouse tower was first commissioned in 1849 and has protected ships from the dangers of Caithness' jagged eastern shores till this day.

After becoming fully automated in 1987, all of the buildings around the lighthouse and the 39 acres of land they were built upon were sold, with the exception of the single white tower, which remained as an active lighthouse. The former building that once housed the lighthouse keeper is now available for guests to enjoy the stunning views of the cliffs and horizon beyond as one of Scotland's most unique accommodation choices.

The accommodation can sleep six people and is fully self-catering, perfect for large family getaways or a quiet retreat to the highlands with those closest to you.
///giggled.inversely.latter

EAT &
STAY
£

SINCLAIR BAY HOTEL, Keiss

As the road winds its way north along the eastern coast of Caithness, the village of Keiss delivers a gratefully accepted resting point for the weary traveller. At the centre of this village sits the warm and welcoming shelter of the Sinclair Bay Hotel, the local watering hole and house to a range of comfortable rooms to rest your head.

This hotel is ideally situated for those exploring Caithness, with the closest beach sitting just over half a mile away, and the fascinating castles of Keiss, Bucholie, and Sinclair Girnigoe all within a 20 minute drive.
///driven.appoints.weekday

STAY
££

HILLSIDE CAMPING PODS, Auckengill

Enjoy a quirky stay in a choice of two glamping pods or a superior shepherd's hut in the remote wilderness of Caithness. Situated in the heart of the natural phenomenon known as the

"Flow Country", these glamping pods are the perfect base to explore the fascinating sights of Europe's largest area of blanket bog.

All of the accommodation options are self-contained and feature all of the necessary kitchen and living essentials to ensure a relaxing and memorable stay. All of the pods have a small kitchenette with a dining area, as well as a private bathroom with a shower. They also contain a microwave, a fridge, toaster, and kettle.
///stun.myself.wage

THE ANCHORAGE B&B, John o' Groats

STAY
£

The Anchorage is a beautiful bed and breakfast situated in John o' Groats. The owners, Gail and Dave are very welcoming and will be great hosts throughout your stay. The Anchorage boasts stunning sea views and is in a perfect location for exploring the surrounding area. There are two guest rooms on the upper floor alongside a large, open-plan lounge and breakfast area.
///rashers.animator.liners

FLAVOURS ICE CREAM AND CONFECTIONERY, John o' Groats

EAT
£

The UK's most northerly ice-cream parlour, Flavours serves up a delicious range of flavours of ice-cream, as well as a host of other tasty confectionery. One of the local favourites is the highly decadent waffle basket, featuring the usual delicious ice-cream, served up in a crunchy waffle bowl and topped with lashings of a sweet treat of your choice. The perfect way to celebrate your journey to the end of mainland UK.
///remarks.invest.deflation

JOHN O' GROATS BY TOGETHER TRAVEL, John o' Groats

STAY
££

One of the most iconic accommodations on the North Coast 500 route, this collection of self-catering apartments is unmistakable, with its colourful facade overlooking the Pentland Firth on Scotland's northeastern tip. The John o' Groats by

The colourful buildings of John o' Groats by Together Travel, John o' Groats

Together Travel offers a range of luxury apartments with stunning views, all for a very reasonable cost. This is the perfect location for whale watching and northern lights spotting all from the comfort of your bedroom.

The choice of accommodation here ranges from a selection of three-bedroom apartments, all with floor-to-ceiling windows facing the sea, to a renovated 19th century inn with one-, two- and four-bedroom apartments. All of the accommodation here has been decorated to perfection, oozing luxury, style, and an unforgettable level of comfort.
///sketching.inviting.statement

JOHN O' GROATS CAMPSITE, John o' Groats

Britain's most northeasterly campsite, the John o' Groats campsite offers a comfortable and affordable place to rest after a long journey north. Just a short walk from one of the UK's most photographed signposts, this is the finishing point of the popular journey that stretches from Britain's most south-westerly point at Land's End in Cornwall. The campsite overlooks the beautiful stretch of water of the Pentland Firth, with views of the Isle of Stroma and onto the Islands of Orkney.

On the four acre site at John o' Groats you will find all of the necessary requirements that can be expected from a campsite of this class. There are a total of 90 hard-standing pitches available, as well as a toilet and shower block, laundry facilities, waste disposal, and plenty of electrical hook-ups for touring vehicles.
///finely.deposits.direction

SEAVIEW HOTEL, John o' Groats

If you are looking for a comfortable place to stay with incredible sea views, then look no further than the Seaview Hotel in John o' Groats. Whether you are looking to stay in a room, a bunkhouse or a pod, Seaview Hotel has you covered with a range of all three accommodation options on site. You can choose from a double, twin or family room or a budget glamping pod that sleeps up to three people with two single beds and a hammock.

At the bar and restaurant you can enjoy freshly cooked meals using locally sourced ingredients based on seasonality. One thing to note is that they don't scrimp on portion sizes!
///sprinkler.swan.deflection

STACKS DELI AND BAKERY, John o' Groats

Established in 2016, this cafe and deli shop sells everything from freshly prepared food and cakes to all forms of locally produced foods, drinks, and souvenirs. Despite this huge range of delicious food, Stacks is famous for its mouth-wateringly good brownies, so much so that they have released their own brownie cookbook.

Be sure to pay a visit here during your trip to Britain's most north-eastern point and if you have a four-legged companion, why not treat them to one of the unique "pupcakes" on sale in Stacks.
///shadowing.jeep.bring

ANNIE'S BAKERY, Upper Gills

Annie's Bakery is a creative and unique bakery located in Wick, near John o' Groats. Annie started the bakery in 2013, however, at that time, she only supplied her goods to shops directly. With a passion for creativity and working with the public, Annie dreamt of opening her own place for people to come and enjoy her creative work, and in 2020 this dream became a reality.

Although hot food is served at lunchtime, it really is the cakes (and, of course, the warm welcome) that are the main attractions of visiting Annie's Bakery.
///impulses.parading.jingles

CASTLE OF MEY CAFÉ, Mey

This grand and beautiful 16th century castle was built by the 4th Earl of Caithness and was passed down through the generations until the 15th Earl of Caithness passed away with no children. After this, it was subsequently sold into royal

Annie's Bakery, Upper Gills

possession and restored and renovated by the Queen Mother in the middle of the 20th century, after which it remained under the care of the Castle of Mey Trust.

Visitors today can explore the internals and externals of the Castle of Mey, including its beautiful walled garden. There is also an onsite visitor centre and cafe where guests can learn about the fascinating history of the region and the part that the Castle of Mey played on it, as well as relax with a brew and some freshly prepared food from the kitchen.
///frog.streak.crumble

STAY
£

WINDHAVEN CAMPING AND B&B, Brough

Windhaven Camping and B&B is the most northerly campsite and B&B on mainland UK. Clare and Phil run the family business, with help from Aunty Babs, and will ensure that you have a welcoming and comfortable stay.

Located only one mile south of Dunnet head, the most northerly point on the mainland, Windhaven Camping and B&B has incredible views across to Orkney and is in a prime location to see the northern lights. Overlooking Brough Bay, you must look out for seals during your time here from the seal viewing point on site.

There are three comfortable B&B rooms with a communal lounge area and a 2.5 acre campsite. From here you will have great views over the Pentland Firth and across to the Orkney Isles.

There is a snack and gift shop onsite selling sandwiches, cakes and tea and coffee.
///biked.refers.invisible

STAY
£

DUNNET BAY CARAVAN AND MOTORHOME CLUB CAMPSITE, Dunnet

Dunnet Bay Caravan and Motorhome Club Campsite is located in one of the most picturesque areas on the north coast of

Scotland. Situated on the banks of the stunning white sandy beach, this campsite is only a two-minute walk down to the sandy, dog-friendly beach.

Dunnet Bay Caravan and Motorhome Club Campsite is a great base for exploring the northern part of Caithness with Dunnet Head and John o' Groats not too far a drive away.
///coached.dentures.dignitary

CASTLETOWN HOTEL, Castletown

EAT & STAY £

What more could you want than a place to stay on the north coast of Scotland that is only a 10-minute walk from the beach? Castletown Hotel is located in the centre of the village of Castletown, close to Thurso and Wick. This hotel is popular for its delicious home-cooked food, served in the restaurant which you can enjoy after a day of exploring.

Castletown Hotel is run by two local brothers who have comfort and relaxation at the heart of their ethos. This 18th century building features 24 en-suite bedrooms, each decorated with Scottish charm and furnished with all that you need for a comfortable stay.
///hooks.chatted.threaded

THE ULBSTER ARMS HOTEL, Halkirk

Situated on the banks of River Thurso in the village of Halkirk, the Ulbster Arms Hotel has stood proudly for over 150 years. Formerly used as a holiday home by the Sinclair family, this grand mansion now offers a comfortable and memorable stay just 10-minutes south of the northern town of Thurso.

With an onsite bar offering a range of hot and cold drinks, free onsite parking and beautiful views from the rooms, this hotel is a fantastic choice for a relaxing stay on the NC500. There is also an onsite restaurant to relax in for breakfast, lunch, or dinner, that focuses on using locally sourced beef, lamb, pork and venison, all reared on the large grassy plains of Caithness.
///attic.trash.metals

A surfer competing at Thurso East, Thurso

BYDAND, Thurso

A great place to eat out in Thurso is Bydand Restaurant, which is situated in the centre of Thurso. This restaurant has a small set menu and serves high quality locally sourced meals catering to a range of dietary requirements.
///charities.hunter.earlobe

THE CROFTER'S SNUG CAMPSITE AND GLAMPING, Thurso

Opened in 2016, this cosy and welcoming glamping, caravan and motorhome site sits just a short drive from the most northerly point of mainland Britain. The Crofter's Snug features three cabins and five hard-standing pitches for touring vehicles, and the entire site boasts stunning sea views over the distant Islands of Orkney and beyond.

Far from the main road between the northern towns of Thurso and John o' Groats, this campsite is the perfect location for a peaceful getaway, with incredible views of the sea. There are plenty of areas for dog walking in the area and the nearest beach is less than a mile away, in addition to the host of local attractions just a short drive away.
///ship.indirect.reclining

THE PARK HOTEL, Thurso

The Park Hotel can be found on the northern coast of the NC500 and is perfectly situated a short walk from Thurso train station. It is also makes an ideal stop-over to sail across to the Orkney Islands as it is only a five-minute drive from Scrabster ferry terminal.

This family owned hotel features clean and comfortable bedrooms, each with a power shower and with many rooms also featuring a bath. There is a bar and restaurant onsite serving a wide selection of delicious meals for lunch and dinner.
///timidly.crafted.opposites

EAT
£££

NC5OO

STAY
£

EAT &
STAY
£

PENNYLAND HOUSE, Thurso

Pennyland House is a historic house that was built in 1780 and was the birthplace of the founder of the Boys' Brigade. It has recently been renovated into a beautiful and relaxing bed and breakfast. Raymond and Carol, the owners of Pennyland House, are local and have lived in Thurso for most of their lives and are therefore very knowledgeable about the area and can provide a lot of helpful advice.

All rooms at Pennyland House are unique, although all have stunning sea views and en-suites, and are named after Raymond's favourite golf courses.
///monorail.muddy.amplifier

NC5⦿0

SANDRA'S BACKPACKERS, Thurso

Sandra's Backpackers is located in the highland town of Thurso within walking distance of shops, bars and restaurants. It is a great base for your trip to the northern highlands, situated near some of the most beautiful beaches and some of the best surf in the UK.

There are a variety of bedrooms featuring bunkbeds and double beds and a bathroom with a toilet and a shower. There is a shared kitchen and a TV and lounge area.
///surpasses.toddler.ventures

SPICE TANDOORI, Thurso

Unwind at the end of a long day exploring the highlands with some delicious and freshly made Indian cuisine from Spice Tandoori in the highland town of Thurso. Highly rated among locals and tourists alike, this restaurant offers either take-away or sit-in dining experiences, all for a very reasonable price.
///cashew.history.upsetting

Strathy Point Lighthouse, near Thurso

173

NC5○○

STATION HOTEL AND APARTMENTS, Thurso

The Station Hotel is located in the highland town of Thurso and hosts 35 bedrooms with single beds, double beds, family rooms and studios. The studio rooms offer more space and a separate sitting area and a desk within the room. As well as a variety of rooms, there are 11 one- and two-bedroom apartments available for long-term lease.

There is a relaxed dining experience at the Station Hotel and Apartments where you can enjoy locally sourced fresh food. Alongside your meal you can enjoy a wee dram or a glass of wine from their extensive drinks selection.
///noted.tabloid.captions

NC5○○

THURSO BAY CAMPSITE, Thurso

Overlooking one of Scotland's most famous stretches of surf sits the four-and-a-half acres of Thurso Bay Campsite. This camping ground features a total of 64 pitches for touring vehicles to come and enjoy its scenic views over the Pentland Firth. Onsite facilities include a shower block and dishwashing and laundry facilities.

If you simply fancy a bite to eat then the onsite restaurant, the Blue Door, is always happy to welcome visitors not staying on the campsite itself. This take-away shop serves up freshly made grub ranging from burgers to home baking, and, of course, some ice-cream by the sea.
///sidelined.hike.dips

CAPTAIN'S GALLEY SEAFOOD RESTAURANT, Scrabster

Seasonal, sustainable, and simple. This is the here at the Captain's Galley Seafood Restaurant in Scrabster. Over the years, owners Jim and Mary Cowie have strived to provide the freshest ingredients and freshest cuisine in the country, sourcing as much of their produce from local suppliers as possible.

The Captain's Galley resides within the renovated building of the old Scrabster Ice House and Salmon Bothy, which was once used to store the fresh catch of the local fisherman. Today, it is known around the country as one of the world's leading seafood restaurants.
///sidelined.thud.finishes

THE FERRY INN HOTEL, Scrabster

EAT &
STAY
££

The Ferry Inn Hotel is located in Scrabster and is the sister hotel of the Weigh Inn in Thurso. There are nine newly refurbished en-suite bedrooms with fantastic views over the Pentland Firth and across to the Orkney Isles. There are also two luxury cottages available to book.

The Ferry Inn Hotel features two bars, Popeye's public bar and a separate, quieter lounge bar. The Upper Deck restaurant boasts some great views over Thurso Bay and Scrabster Harbour. It is well known for serving up the most succulent, locally sourced steaks and fresh fish and seafood.
///cattle.forwarded.regrowth

PEERIE CAFE, Scrabster

EAT
£

Peerie Cafe can be found in Scrabster, near the well-known town of Thurso. This cafe is a great stop if you are taking the ferry across to Orkney as it is only a 5-minute walk from the ferry terminal. The friendly staff will make you feel welcomed on your visit to Peerie Cafe.
///fits.hang.framework

Sea stacks at Duncansby Head

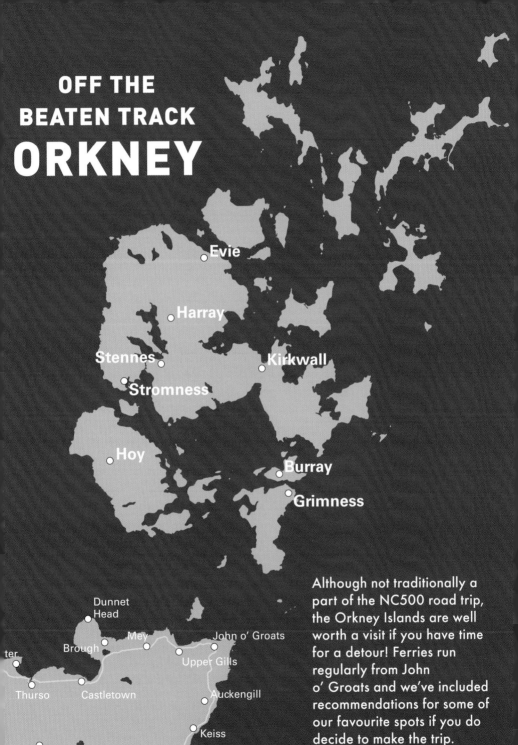

OFF THE
BEATEN TRACK
ORKNEY

Evie

Harray

Stennes

Kirkwall

Stromness

Hoy

Burray

Grimness

Dunnet
Head

Mey

John o' Groats

ter

Brough

Upper Gills

Thurso

Castletown

Auckengill

Halkirk

Keiss

Noss Head

Although not traditionally a part of the NC500 road trip, the Orkney Islands are well worth a visit if you have time for a detour! Ferries run regularly from John o' Groats and we've included recommendations for some of our favourite spots if you do decide to make the trip.

Kirkwall Castle, Kirkwall

ARCHIVE COFFEE, Kirkwall

If you are looking for a unique place to eat out in Orkney, Archive Coffee is the place to go. There is a delicious selection of food on the menu, catering for a variety of requirements including gourmet vegetarian and vegan dishes. There is a bustling, friendly atmosphere in Archive Coffee, with its low beams and quirky decorations bringing the place to life.

Whether you wish to visit to try some of its delicious and off-the-wall food styles, or just want to enjoy a drink with friends, Archive Coffee is the perfect place for you.
///sued.schooling.fruit

AYRE HOTEL & APARTMENTS, Kirkwall

Dating back as far as 1791, the Ayre Hotel and Apartments has been serving visitors to the Orkney Isles for hundreds of years. Throughout this time, the hotel has grown in popularity and now it is widely known as one of the finest accommodations of its kind in the region. This family run business consists of the original hotel building, as well as newly constructed, self-catering apartments next door to it.

The hotel has an onsite bar and restaurant to entertain and satisfy the guests and the public, offering a range of locally sourced ingredients and a creative range of vegetarian and vegan options.
///boomers.sudden.plankton

BUSTER'S DINER, Kirkwall

A unique dining experience on the island of Orkney, Buster's Diner is an American-themed diner, complete with everything from the retro decor to the friendly American charm. Buster's Diner serves up a selection of classic pub meals and other American meals, from pizzas to burgers. The well-stocked bar also has a range of delicious Orkney beers for you to try with your meal.
///wrenching.eliminate.gardens

THE FOVERAN, Kirkwall

This traditional Scottish restaurant is run by two local Orcadian families who split the roles of running such a business evenly among them. This intimate division of the business reflects perfectly in the quality of service that you can expect here at the Foveran.

Rated as a 4-star restaurant with rooms by Visit Scotland, the Foveran has everything from spectacular views of Scapa Flow to delicious and fresh food on the menu, as well as a selection of luxurious rooms that are available to rent. The attention to detail in each of the rooms, the passion that goes into the food that is served, and most of all the friendliness of the staff, have all resulted in a huge number of return visitors for the Foveran and incredible reviews online.
///whisk.playfully.daily

KIRKWALL BAY TOURING PARK, Kirkwall

This shoreside campsite lies just over a mile to the north of the principal town of Kirkwall and boasts incredible views over the water to the north of the Orkney mainland. The Kirkwall Bay Touring Park contains its own heated shower block and toilet facilities, as well as indoor washing and laundry facilities. It is the perfect location for anyone looking for somewhere to camp close to the sea and within easy access of the bustling streets of Kirkwall.
///bother.unrated.limitless

ORKNEY CARAVAN PARK AT THE PICKAQUOY CENTRE, Kirkwall

The largest caravan park on the island of Orkney, the Pickaquoy complex offers an excellent choice for those wanting home comforts and easy access to the town of Kirkwall. This 4-star campsite has a range of facilities, including electric hookups, hard-standing pitches, waste disposal and water collection and a modern utilities block with a kitchen, toilets, showers, and washing facilities. There is also a choice of two camping pods for those who do not have a tent of their own or for anyone wanting some solid walls for the night.

The Storehouse, Kirkwall

The campsite is just a short walk from the high street of Kirkwall, the busiest town on Orkney and the best place to visit if you are looking for delicious food and great atmosphere.
///knee.marketing.sailed

THE ORKNEY HOTEL, Kirkwall

In the year of 1670, a local merchant of Orkney, Mr John Richan, built his family home in the town of Kirkwall. Over the next two centuries, the family home remained with the Richans as they continued with the family business of litstering (dyeing). Eventually, the house was sold at some point in the 19th century and became an inn to welcome travellers visiting the remote islands.

To this day, this hotel has continued this custom and welcomes visitors to Orkney with its warm Orcadian hospitality and quaint charms that have been protected over the years. Despite the many renovations that the hotel has experienced through the years, there are still sections of the hotel that reflect the original house of Mr John Richan, such as the remnants of the original archway that can be found to the left of the hotel's main entrance.
///kinder.broken.confining

STOREHOUSE, Kirkwall

The Storehouse is a unique hotel and dining experience in the small town of Kirkwall on the Isle of Orkney. This modern hotel was opened in 2018 and features 14 tables and a restaurant and bar area. The friendly staff will welcome you to the Storehouse with open arms and you can expect a comfortable and peaceful stay, paired with a delicious, freshly cooked meal.

The onsite restaurant is open to the public and is a very popular choice with locals and tourists alike, with tables here at the Storehouse quickly booking up. There is also a cosy fireplace by the door with some very comfortable chairs if all you fancy is a warm place to enjoy a drink.
///loves.signs.subject

SUNBEAN COFFEE HOUSE, Kirkwall

EAT
£

A warm and welcoming cafe serving up freshly roasted coffee beans and homemade cakes, the SunBean Coffee House can be found in the centre of Kirkwall, just along the road from the historic St Magnus Cathedral. As well as some of the best coffee in Orkney, the SunBean Coffee House also sells a range of more unique hot drinks, such as turmeric chai lattes, and a range of caffeine-free alternatives.
///firelight.heartache.clinked

TWENTY ONE, Kirkwall

EAT
£

A fully licensed bar and restaurant on the High Street of Kirkwall, Twenty One is a fantastic place to enjoy a refreshing drink and a delicious meal in the heart of Orkney. Open Monday to Saturday, Twenty One serves up a range of lunches during the day and small plates during the evenings later in the week. The tasteful interior decor and creative cocktail menu make it a fun and lively spot to spend the evening after a day out exploring Orkney.
///proclaims.wipe.richest

STONEHIGH CAMPSITE, Evie

STAY
£

Just one mile from the nearest beach, Stonehigh Campsite is located in the northwest of the mainland of Orkney. Far from the nearby towns, Stonehigh is set on a working farm and is a popular spot for bird-watching, with frequent sightings of kestrels, short-eared owls, and hen harriers.

This site is perfect for those looking for a relaxing escape to the countryside, with its peaceful setting and lack of any nearby shops, pubs or restaurants.
///reacting.young.feasted

THE SKERRIES RESTAURANT, Harray

EAT
££

Dine out in this unique "all-glass" bistro cafe that overlooks the beautiful Loch of Harray in the west of Orkney. The owners of the Skerries Restaurant, Carole and Hamish Mowatt, make it their daily goal to serve up the freshest seafood that the Isle of Orkney has to offer, sourcing it from the nearest harbour that sits just two miles away and preparing all of the fish themselves.

Ring of Brodgar, Stenness

In addition to the range of fresh seafood on offer here, the team at the Skerries also prepares all bread, cakes and desserts in-house as well, the perfect excuse to enjoy something sweet with a coffee and the stunning view of Orkney through the floor-to-ceiling windows.
///blacked.plankton.fights

THE STANDING STONES HOTEL, Stenness

EAT &
STAY
££

Lose yourself in the wonder of the Neolithic side of Orkney, from ancient standing stones to entire settlements perfectly preserved in time. The Standing Stones Hotel overlooks the Loch of Stenness and onto the manmade phenomenon of the Ring of Brodgar. The hotel is also in easy reach of other ancient wonders, such as the Standing Stones of Stenness, as well as the other UNESCO sites around the island.

The Standing Stones Hotel offers a comfortable and welcoming accommodation option with an onsite restaurant and bar, free breakfast for all guests, and beautiful views from the front windows over the water.
///brotherly.bond.impulsive

THE FERRY INN, Stromness

EAT &
STAY
£££

Overlooking the ancient ferryport of Stromness, the aptly named Ferry Inn has been welcoming visitors off the boats for over 30 years. The award-winning bar, named "The Ferry" has always proved to be a thriving social hub for the locals of Orkney, hosting special events and festivals over the years.

The Ferry Inn has 18 rooms to offer in the main building itself, which is located directly across from the ferry terminal of Stromness. In addition to this, newly developed self-catering apartments are now situated just beside the Ferry Inn and are perfect for larger parties or for anyone wanting the privacy of their own space.
///delight.obstruct.compress

EAT
£££

HAMNAVOE RESTAURANT, Stromness

Named after the old Nordic word for Stromness, aka "Haven Bay" or "Safe Harbour", the Hamnavoe Restaurant serves up the freshest catch from the bay with a range of high quality seafood on the menu. This highly rated restaurant sits in the southerly town of Stromness, one of the ferry ports that connects Orkney with mainland UK.

As with any fresh produce, the catch of the day varies on a day-to-day basis and so does the menu, however, on a visit to the Hamnavoe you can expect seafood such as prawn and shrimp, sole, monkfish, and halibut. The skilled in-house chefs also provide choices to those who do not fancy seafood, with turf and vegetarian options available as well.
///shelving.witty.whimpered

EAT
£

JULIA'S CAFE BISTRO, Stromness

Across from the Stromness ferry terminal, one of Orkney's main links to the mainland of the UK, sits the small cafe known as Julia's Cafe Bistro. This is the perfect place to grab a bite to eat or a coffee to go if you are either arriving or leaving the island of Orkney, or if you fancy a meal in the sunshine, there is a handful of outdoor seats available. Choose from a selection of hot filled rolls, teas and coffees, fresh salad boxes, freshly baked cakes, and locally made Orkney ice-cream.
///sway.share.grad

STAY
££

POINT OF NESS CARAVAN & CAMPING SITE, Stromness

Perched on the southerly point of the town of Stromness, the Point of Ness Campsite sits right on the shoreline of Scapa Flow and has incredible views of the surrounding islands of Hoy and Graemsay. The campsite has a total of 42 pitches with 28 electrical hookups, as well as a toilet and shower block complete with washing and drying facilities.

One of the most popular aspects of the Point of Ness campsite is its close proximity to the town of Stromness, with the main harbour sitting just a 20 minute walk away. This makes it the

Skara Brae, Orkney

perfect place to pitch-up for the night and enjoy the live music in the small harbour town.
///unhelpful.enveloped.pass

EAT
£

SKARA BRAE CAFE, Stromness

Over 5,000 years ago, the small settlement of Skara Brae was alive with laughter and joy. This ancient Neolithic settlement is one of the best preserved of its kind in the whole of Europe, and it is possible for you to walk among the ruins and become a part of that history.

The Skara Brae Visitor Centre gives access to the ruins of Skara Brae, a site that was rediscovered in 1850 after a large storm, and has since become a site of extreme archaeological significance. At this site it is possible to see the original, 5000-year-old furniture that would have been used, to peer inside the nine remaining houses that still stand today, and to see the fascinating artefacts that were discovered here over the years, such as the jewellery that once was worn by the inhabitants.

On this site there is also a small cafe for visitors to enjoy some refreshments after a morning of exploring this wonder of Scotland.
///baker.lace.clutter

STAY
££

THE STROMNESS HOTEL, Stromness

Opened in 1901, this historic hotel has served the town of Stromness for over 100 years, welcoming visitors from the ferry to Orkney and providing a comfortable bed for the night for weary explorers. The hotel consists of 42 bedrooms, each equipped with the basic amenities that you would expect from a 3-star accommodation, such as a TV and tea and coffee-making facilities. There is also the option to choose a room with views over the historical Stromness Harbour, the open water of Scapa Flow beyond.
///tastes.senders.giant

BENETH'ILL CAFE, Hoy

EAT
£

A remote cafe, located on the smaller island of Hoy – part of the Orkney archipelago – is the small and quaint Beneth'Ill Cafe. Situated inside an old traditional Scottish bothy structure, with a low, sloped roof and thick stone walls, and with views over the wildernesses Hoy and Orkney, the Beneth'Ill Cafe is about as Scottish as it comes.

The cafe serves up a selection of hot drinks, filled rolls, toasted paninis and sandwiches, home-baked goods, such as cakes and scones, and a huge selection of locally sourced beers. ///milkman.gone.withdraws

POLLY KETTLE, Burray

EAT
£

The small tearoom of the Polly Kettle sits on the island between South Ronaldsay and mainland Orkney, with stunning views of the crystal clear waters and white sand beaches that the Orkney islands are famous for.

What began as a small pottery shop has since expanded into a bustling coffee shop, which is hugely popular with the locals, where you can not only enjoy a fresh coffee and delicious cake, but also browse the beautiful collection of local crafts that are produced by hand right here on Orkney. Many of the pieces of pottery artwork that you will find here were made by hand by the incredibly talented owner, Mohammed.

The owners of the Polly Kettle, Linda and Mohammed, decided to open the Polly Kettle after a visit to the islands in 2014 stole their hearts and inspired them to move here soon after. Since then, they have worked tirelessly to create a cosy and welcoming environment where everyone can come together to celebrate good food, beautiful views, and the local spirit that is so cherished here on these northern islands. ///watched.squashes.discussed

Polly Kettle, Burray

THE SANDS HOTEL, Burray

The 19th century structure of the Sands Hotel sits on the banks of the famous waters of Scapa Flow. This building was originally used as a herring store where the freshly caught fish would be stored and packed, ready for transport off island to their final destinations. Throughout the following centuries, its uses changed with the owners, later becoming a coal store facility, then self-catering apartments, a bar and lounge, and finally a 4-star hotel in the late 20th century.

The hotel sits just south of the famous Churchill Barriers, the causeways that stretch from the northern isles of Orkney to South Ronaldsay. This stretch of road is a stunning place to visit, with crystal clear water lapping on white sand beaches, and the shipwreck of the former German Steamer known as the Ilsenstein, which was sunk here during the Second World War as a way of blocking this passage before the barriers were installed.

The Sands Hotel offers a range of rooms, from classic en-suites to king-sized rooms, all fitted with the home comforts you expect, such as a kettle, hairdryer, and biscuits on arrival. There is also an onsite bar and restaurant with a large menu for lunch and dinner, including a dedicated vegan/vegetarian menu.
///additives.coconut.greet

POOL FARMHOUSE CAMPSITE, Grimness

A quiet, adults-only campsite in South Ronaldsay with breathtaking views of the eastern coast of Scapa Flow. The Pool Farmhouse is a small and intimate setting, with just five touring sites available. The site is simple and comfortable, with all of the basic necessities that you would expect from a touring site, such as waste disposal and water collection, as well as electric hookups. There are no toilets or shower facilities.
///premises.flirts.correctly

WESTER ROSS

Lairg

Rosehall

Torroble

Brora

Invershin

Golspie

Bonar Bridge

Embo

Ardgay

Evelix

Dornoch

Edderton

Portmahomack

Tain

Fearn

Ardross

Balintore

Delny

Nigg

Alness

Invergordon

Evanton

Cromarty

Garve

Dingwall

Rosemarkie

Strathpeffer

Fortrose

Munlochy

Avoch

Muir of Ord

Kessock

Beauly

Inverness

Cannich

A view across the water at the Altnacealgach Inn, Lairg

THE ALTNACEALGACH MOTEL, Lairg

The Altnacealgach Motel is located in Lairg on the north-west coast of Scotland. The en-suite rooms are modern with a fully equipped kitchenette and seating area with a TV. The Altnacealgach Inn is situated next door where you can enjoy a delicious breakfast or evening meal. There is a lot to explore in the surrounding area including the Bone Caves and the Knockan Crag Nature Reserve.
///cheetahs.fled.feasts

EAT & STAY ££

ARDMAIR POINT HOLIDAY PARK, Ardmair

Ardmair Point Holiday Park is located on the banks of a sea loch, three miles north of Ullapool. Most of the pitches on the Holiday Park have a stunning view out to sea, overlooking a pebbled bay with access to the water and, when the weather is right, you can witness the most incredible sunset past the Summer Isles and the Outer Hebrides.

Ardmair Point Holiday Park sits on a peninsula, with one side a touring caravan and camping park and the other side being self-catering accommodation that includes chalets, lodges and a holiday home. There are great facilities onsite including a coffee shop and small shop for your convenience.
///gained.metals.amounting

STAY ££

NCS5◎○

THE HIGHLAND BOTHIES, Morefield

The Highland Bothies are a luxury Glamping experience hosted by Ruth and Iain MacLennan on their working croft. Overlooking Loch Broom, the two micro-lodges, "An Teallach" and "Beinn Ghobhlach", are elevated to give unspoilt panoramic views and each lodge has a private patio area and hot tub. Wild deer often roam around the area and you may also see some magnificent birds of prey flying around too. After a day of exploring the surrounding area, come home to the peace and tranquillity of your lodge, cook up a barbecue, light up the fire pit and do a bit of stargazing.
///warms.loved.defaults

STAY £

NCS5◎○

ARDVRECK HOUSE HOTEL, Ullapool

Sitting just outside of the highland town of Ullapool, Ardvreck House Hotel is situated overlooking the banks of Loch Broom and surrounded by the mountains. There are ten bedrooms in the hotel varying from single, twin and double rooms, and all rooms feature their own en-suite bathroom. Each bedroom is uniquely decorated and has a beautiful view from the window.

There is a shared lounge area and a dining room where you can enjoy a delicious breakfast with a magnificent panoramic view.

Ardvreck House Hotel is a great base for exploring the Ullapool area.
///dispenser.escalated.tank

BROOMFIELD HOLIDAY PARK, Ullapool

Broomfield Holiday Park is set on the banks of Loch Broom and has been welcoming visitors to Ullapool for over 60 years. The holiday park is within walking distance of the town of Ullapool where you will find many bars, restaurants and shops and other things to do around the town, such as Ullapool hill. It is also a great base for those wishing to visit the Outer Hebrides, as the ferry port is in the centre of town.

Broomfield Holiday Park is the only campsite within easy walking distance of Ullapool and it extends over 12 acres, overlooking the most incredible views of the Summer Isles and Loch Broom.

There are great facilities onsite for campers, including laundry facilities and a dish-washing area.
///fuses.debit.betraying

CEILIDH PLACE, Ullapool

A favourite place to dine in the heart of Ullapool is the Ceilidh Place, a cafe and hotel and bunkhouse.

Ceilidh Place, Ullapool

Established in 1970 by Robert Urquhart, a well known Scottish actor, the Ceilidh Place was opened as a place where people could gather. The ethos at the Ceilidh Place is strong on traditional songs, poetry and art and features exhibitions from local artists. The cafe serves a delicious selection of cakes and coffees as well as hot food. All ingredients are sourced as locally as possible.

The hotel has 13 unique rooms and a resident's lounge with a small kitchen area and balcony. There is also a bunkhouse providing budget hostel style private rooms.
///without.fended.roadblock

EAT &
STAY
£££

THE DIPPING LUGGER, Ullapool
A highly recommended boutique restaurant with rooms, the Dipping Lugger is one of the most unique experiences in the region of Ullapool. Using everything from the ingredients on the plate to the history of the building itself, every dining experience tells the story of the history and significance of the town of Ullapool to the surrounding areas.

The Dipping Lugger also has three beautiful rooms for guests to enjoy as a luxurious and memorable stay overlooking the bonnie banks of Loch Broom.
///clearing.forgives.scanty

EAT &
STAY
£

FERRY BOAT INN, Ullapool
Just a short walk from the ferry terminal in the busy highland town of Ullapool is the traditional seafood restaurant with rooms, known as the Ferry Boat Inn. As one of the highland's largest harbour towns, there aren't many better places to try the freshest seafood in the region.

Above the restaurant and bar, the Ferry Boat Inn has a selection of rooms for those who would like to spend the night in this vibrant harbour town. From single rooms to doubles with a lochside view, this inn has it all.
///engaging.croutons.biked

ROYAL HOTEL, Ullapool

Believed to be the oldest continually used hotel in the bustling town of Ullapool, the Royal Hotel is one of the premier luxury hotels in the region of Wester Ross. With 55 rooms for visitors to enjoy, a cosy bar with a great selection of whiskies, and a delicious menu on offer in the onsite restaurant, the Royal Hotel is the perfect place to relax and unwind on the west coast of Scotland.

///lordship.moment.early

SEAFOOD SHACK, Ullapool

A unique open-air diner in the heart of the harbour town of Ullapool, the Seafood Shack serves up the best fresh catch of the day that the town has to offer. Since 2015, the team at the Seafood Shack have been showing Ullapool the joys of simply cooked seafood that can be enjoyed with friends in the summer sun.

Owners of the shack, Kirsty and Fenella, are both local to the highlands of Scotland. Kirsty was born and raised in Ullapool and Fenella comes from the more southerly village of Achmore. Both with personal experience with loved ones in the fishing industry, they decided to pursue their passion in creating great food with a stunning backdrop to admire it with. With this as their motivation, the Seafood Shack was born.

Over the following decade, the number of features and awards that the Seafood Shack has enjoyed has tallied up and the popularity of the stall has grown, making it difficult to even find a seat on a sunny day in Ullapool.

///debit.cushy.rooks

THE SEAFORTH BAR AND RESTAURANT, Ullapool

For over 160 years, the Seaforth Bar and Restaurant has stood in the town of Ullapool. It has been used through the decades as a fish and coal store for the local fishing boats and steamboats, as a chandlery for the boats and harbour, and as a smokehouse for the fresh catch.

The Seaforth Bar and Restaurant, Ullapool

Eventually, it was transformed into a pub and inn and began serving up the fresh seafood that it had played a crucial part in catching for so long. Since then, the Seaforth has become one of Ullapool's premium bars and restaurants, always bustling with popularity and thriving with a great atmosphere.

With an outdoor patio area offering panoramic views of the harbour and Loch Broom, the bar and restaurant is always the perfect place to end a day out in Scotland, with a hearty meal on the plate and a local beer in hand.
///redouble.twitches.bandwagon

THE STONEHOUSES ULLAPOOL, Ullapool

STAY
£££

The Stonehouses in Ullapool are two unique luxurious properties on the west coast of Scotland that overlook Loch Broom and the surrounding mountains from an elevated level. Curved Stone is one of the properties at the Stonehouses and it features a double bedroom with an en-suite and a twin bedroom. The modern interior is neutral and stylish and the large windows create a light and spacious feel. The panoramic windows open up to magical views across Loch Broom and the dramatic mountains, not to forget the incredible sunsets that can be seen from here and the external seating area.

Treetop is the second accommodation at The Stonehouses, which is also elevated on the hill with views of Loch Broom and surrounded by forestry. This self-catering accommodation has two double bedrooms, one of which has an en-suite and a freestanding bath. Underneath the Treetop is a gorge which after heavy rainfall, turns into a full-flowing waterfall.

Both accommodations are perfect for a romantic getaway on the NC500.
///slopes.material.defenders

ULLAPOOL YOUTH HOSTEL, Ullapool

STAY
£

Ullapool Youth Hostel is a great base to stay, surrounded as it is by iconic mountains and with beautiful views across Loch Broom and the Beinn Dearg mountain. Ullapool is a fishing village in the highlands, with connections to the Outer Hebrides and Stornoway, and has plenty of shops, bars and restaurants.

There are a variety of rooms available at the Ullapool Youth Hostel, including private and shared rooms. One of the private rooms has an en-suite and the others have access to shared bathroom facilities. Onsite, you will find a well-equipped kitchen with a comfortable lounge area to relax in after a day of exploring.

The Ullapool Youth Hostel has bike storage available as well as laundry and drying facilities.
///selection.desks.active

STAY
££

WESTLEA HOUSE BOUTIQUE B&B, Ullapool
Westlea House Boutique B&B is a quirky accommodation located within walking distance of the town centre of Ullapool. It features five unique and comfortable bedrooms and a shared lounge and dining area. In the lounge there is a cosy wood-burner, books and vinyl records.

The first floor has three unique rooms of different sizes and the second floor has two further rooms. All rooms feature luxurious en-suite facilities, with powerful showers and two of the rooms feature a freestanding Victorian-style slipper bath. All bedrooms have stylish furnishings, free WIFI and a TV.

Terry and Shirley will make you feel very welcome in their home and offer some great breakfast options in the morning of your stay.
///procures.enveloped.sticking

STAY
££

SEALOCH HOUSE, Loggie
Sealoch House is a modern, eco-friendly house with stunning views across Loch Broom near the highland town of Ullapool. The open-plan design and large windows make for a very comfortable living space that has everything you need for a peaceful and relaxing experience. In the lounge there is a wood-burner that creates a cosy ambiance and large doors out to the wooden decking with magnificent views across Loch Broom.

Ullapool Harbour, Ullapool

Sealoch House sleeps six people across three beautiful bedrooms complete with high quality en-suites. It is also fully equipped with a stylish kitchen and complete with a washing machine and tumble dryer.
///skews.revised.distanced

EAT & STAY ££

DUNDONNELL HOTEL, Dundonnell
The Dundonnell Hotel is a family run hotel that sits on the shores of Little Loch Broom at the foot of the mountain, An Teallach. There are 23 comfortable en-suite rooms ranging from single to family rooms with mountain or loch views.

There is a coffee shop onsite where you can enjoy the delicious home-baked cakes and pastries. If you enjoy folk music, then you will love the regular live music sessions that take place in the Broombeg Bar at the Dundonnell Hotel. You can join in or you can sit and listen and enjoy. The Broombeg Bar also serves as a restaurant with some tasty, locally sourced dishes.
///divide.flips.organisms

STAY £

NC500

GRUINARD BAY CARAVAN PARK, Laide
Gruinard Bay Caravan Park lies north of Gairloch and Poolewe, south of Ullapool and is a stunning place to stay. There are five rental caravans and many grass and hard-standing touring pitches along the seafront, each pitch fenced off to allow for privacy and additional shelter. This area is well known for being peaceful and tranquil with incredible views out to sea. The beach is a short walk from the campsite and there is a small village shop and petrol station nearby.

Keep a look out for seals and otters along the shoreline and if the weather is right, you could see a cracking sunset.
///vitamins.joined.originate

STAY £££

BLISS HAUS, Ormiscaig
Bliss Haus is a spectacular unique accommodation in Wester Ross offering magical views of the surrounding scenery. This self-catering accommodation sleeps four, with one double

bedroom and one bunk bedroom for children. There is a fully equipped kitchen and a beautiful dining area with a sunset glitter ball supplying a golden light disco as the sun sets.

Bliss Haus has floor-to-ceiling length windows surrounding the living space, connecting you with nature as you are provided with stunning views of Loch Ewe and across to the Outer Hebrides. The bold design is incredibly stylish and makes for a very relaxing environment. Sustainability has been considered, allowing you to have a trendy break away with a low carbon footprint.
///dandelions.lengthen.inflates

BRIDGE COTTAGE CAFE, Poolewe
Situated just off the main street of Poolewe, the cosy, family run Bridge Cottage Cafe welcomes guests with the enticing smell of freshly baked bread and mouthwatering cakes. This is a popular stop-off for travellers passing through the village of Poolewe as a place to fuel up after a morning of adventures with the highly popular sourdough breads and baguettes. As well as the cosy internal seating, the cafe also has external seating for guests to enjoy the warmer weather.
///suggested.file.skippers

EAT
£

CORRINESS HOUSE, Poolewe
Located in the picturesque village of Poolewe is Corriness House, a perfect place to stay on your NC500 trip. Ross and Louise Maclean are the couple that own Corriness House and offer a range of accommodation to suit your needs.

STAY
££

The charming Victorian Guest House features six en-suite bedrooms that vary in size from twin- to super-king rooms. Each stay includes a full Scottish or continental breakfast the following morning after arrival.

The Bothy is a self-catering property located at the back of the main house. It is an open-plan yet cosy area with a log-burning fire and mezzanine that sleeps two adults.

Inverewe Gardens, Poolewe

If you are travelling the NC500 as a family or with a larger group, the Cottage at Corriness sleeps up to six people and has access to a garden. The cottage has a beautiful modern interior with three bedrooms, a fully equipped kitchen and laundry facilities.
///undulation.emeralds.sensitive

INVEREWE GARDENS, Poolewe

Inverewe Gardens is a National Trust site with a history dating back to the 19th century. There is a great initiative here for reducing waste and recycling produce and products used. The cafe at Inverewe Gardens is no different in that even the plate that you will eat your lunch from will be made from recycled compost and when you are finished it will be broken down to be used again.

Take a break from wandering around the gardens to enjoy a cuppa and something delicious to eat in Inverewe Gardens tea rooms.
///animated.lifeboats.proofread

POOLEWE HOTEL, Poolewe

Poolewe Hotel is situated on the shore of Loch Ewe and dates back to the 16th century. There are 13 comfortable en-suite bedrooms and suites in the hotel, featuring tea and coffee facilities, a TV and many with windows looking out to the mountains or to Loch Ewe.

There is a restaurant that caters for vegetarian, vegan and gluten-free dietary requirements and a bright conservatory dining space. The public lounge areas feature log fires giving a cosy feel to this historic building.

There are many great things to do near Poolewe Hotel, such as the Inverewe Gardens and Pool House.
///forms.inert.ascendant

ROASTER'S HIGHLAND COFFEE BOX, Poolewe

This small coffee box can be found on the main road of the village of Poolewe, overlooking the tranquil waters of Loch Ewe. Serving speciality Portuguese coffee, along with other decadent treats such as Belgian Hot Chocolate, Spanish Churros, and fresh, hand-pulled sourdough pizzas cooked in the wood-fired oven.

Stop off and say hello to the team at Roaster's Highland Coffee Box and grab a bite to eat with the stunning view over the Poolewe shoreline.
///snowmen.mentions.thickens

FIONN CROFT LODGE AND SHEPHERDS HUT, Melvaig

If you are looking for a peaceful stay in a remote area, Fionn Croft will be right up your street. Choose between spending the night in the family friendly lodge or in a romantic couple's retreat in the cosy shepherd's hut.

Both accommodations boast stunning views of the Scottish coastline and are sure to immerse you in nature.
///dispensed.enabling.ambition

BEACHCOMBER FISH & CHIPS, Gairloch

The local eatery in the small town of Gairloch, this family run fish and chips shop serves up the finest seafood in classic Scottish style. Finish off a day out in Scotland the correct way: grab a fish supper and enjoy it by the seaside with a sunset to remember.
///lawns.destiny.motivations

CRUMBS, Gairloch

A small family run takeaway in Gairloch selling the most delicious selection of homemade soup, sandwiches and cakes. A popular choice for vegetarians is the vegetarian haggis, paired with your choice of cheese in a panini. Delicious!
///clearly.paddlers.chief

The village of Poolewe in Wester Ross

THE GAIRLOCH HOTEL, Gairloch

The Gairloch Hotel is one of most scenic hotels in the area with views overlooking the beach and across to the Isle of Skye, a magical view when the sun sets. This is a great place to base yourself for exploring this part of Scotland.

There are 72 bedrooms, each with an en-suite bathroom and tea and coffee making facilities. The premier rooms feature a four-poster bed with incredible views.

Downstairs, there is a large refurbished restaurant area that serves a delicious selection of European dishes.
///sends.unspoiled.duos

GAIRLOCH SANDS HOSTEL, Gairloch

Gairloch Sands Youth Hostel sits on the northern shore of Loch Gairloch, with panoramic views over Gairloch and the Torridon hills. On a clear day, these magnificent views extend over to the Cuillins on the Isle of Skye and the Outer Hebrides.

There are shared and private rooms available in the hostel with a shared bathroom and a laundry and drying room for your wet clothes. There is a well-equipped self-catering kitchen area or you can opt for the 'Wee Breakfast'. The reception sells basic provisions or a short 15 minute walk will take you to the nearest shop in Gairloch.
///rules.regretted.hamster

GALE CENTRE, Gairloch

The GALE (Gairloch and Loch Ewe Action Forum) centre hosts a community led cafe and gift shop in Gairloch on the west coast of Scotland. This community project promotes economic, social, and environmental benefits to the residents of the local area around Gairloch. The friendly staff serve you at your table whether you choose to sit inside or outside and the menu offers a delicious selection of hot food, cakes and hot drinks.

With sea views across to the Isle of Skye, this friendly cafe is a great place to stop off on your trip.
///kebab.pebbles.mavericks

MOUNTAIN COFFEE CO., Gairloch

The Mountain Coffee Co. is a small coffee shop in Gairloch with a South American style. The hot chocolate is delightfully paired with a seat outside on their patio area overlooking Strath Bay. There is a selection of cakes on offer that you can enjoy alongside your coffee and attached to the cafe is a bookshop that you can have a look around in too.
///twin.sprouted.blotting

EAT
£

MYRTLE BANK HOTEL, Gairloch

Myrtle Bank Hotel, also known as The Myrtle, sits on the seafront in Gairloch showcasing incredible views across the water to the Isle of Sky and the Outer Hebrides. Many of the bedrooms in the hotel also feature this view from the window, and each room has a unique size and design. All bedrooms have an en-suite and the luxury suite has its own lounge area.

The restaurant has an extensive menu featuring seasonal, locally sourced produce including freshly caught seafood. There is a dining terrace where you can enjoy the magnificent views and if you are lucky, you might catch an incredible sunset.

The Myrtle is within close walking distance to stunning white sandy beaches and is only a short drive to many great trails and walks.
///justifies.input.skill

EAT &
STAY
££

THE OLD INN, Gairloch

The Old Inn is located near Gairloch harbour and serves up delicious meals using locally sourced produce. Seafood, such as lobster, mussels, scallops and langoustines are caught and delivered daily from the harbour. As well as the restaurant, The Old Inn now has a Smokehouse and Delicatessen where you can purchase freshly baked bread and croissants and pick up some pre-made seafood sandwiches for your lunch.
///bullion.backhand.credit

EAT &
STAY
££

NC500

Loch Gairloch, Gairloch

SANDS CARAVAN AND CAMPING, Gairloch

Sands Caravan and Camping is a brilliant campsite by the seaside and near the highland village of Gairloch. It is a great base for exploring the local area of Wester Ross. On site there is a licenced shop where you can purchase your groceries and fresh bread is available every morning.

You will have the freedom to choose where you park up at Sands Caravan and Camping as the site is divided into two main areas, one for camping and one for caravans. Big Sand Beach is an award-winning beach and is only a short walk away.

There are plenty of walks close to the site and a short drive will lead you to the spectacular Torridon mountain range.
///cake.limbs.forwarded

BADACHRO INN, Badachro

The Badachro Inn has some of the most scenic views on the west coast of Scotland. The staff and owners are extremely friendly and will make your experience in this part of Scotland a memorable one. There is a great selection of specials on the menu, including those to suit special dietary requirements.

Outside of the restaurant is the Stag and Dough, where you can order a wonderful wood-fired pizza to enjoy on the decking area overlooking the loch.
///could.implanted.noises

DRY ISLAND, Badachro

Dry Island is a unique stay in the area of Badachro, surrounded by the incredible Torridon Mountains where you can experience the tranquillity of the north-west coast of the Scottish Highlands.

There is a floating bridge from the car park that will lead you across to the island where there are three unique self-catering accommodations that each sleep two people. The Old Curing Station is part of the main house and has a hot tub with amazing sea views outside. The Otter Cabin is situated on a secluded part of the island with uninterrupted views of the surrounding scenery. It also features a hot tub to relax in and enjoy the views from.

Lastly, the Captains Cabin and Barrel is a cosy wooden cabin on a private area of the island that features a hot tub with fantastic views. A truly unique place to stay while you are visiting Wester Ross.
///crouches.cling.overlaid

LITTLE AIRD HILL, Badachro

Little Aird Hill offers a home-from-home experience in the small village of Badachro, near Gairloch. This timber-built chalet is complete with a modern, stylish interior with plenty of floor length windows for a beautiful light space. The self-catering property is open-plan with a fully equipped kitchen and a wood-burning stove. The bedroom features a king-sized bed and tasteful decor. This accommodation is on site of the Badachro Distillery and is within close walking distance of the Badachro Inn.
///impaired.positions.uncouth

The Beinn Eighe range, near Kinlochewe

LOCH MAREE HOTEL, Talladale

The Loch Maree Hotel was built in 1872 and sits on the banks of Loch Maree. It welcomes guests to stay in one of their comfortable and cosy rooms on their trip to Wester Ross. The hotel has a restaurant onsite which is open to both residents and non-residents. This is a great place to stay on the NC500 route if you are a keen walker or fisher as there is plenty to do in the area.

///repeated.ducks.cushy

LEDGOWAN LODGE HOTEL, Achnasheen

Ledgowan Lodge Hotel is a Victorian Country House located in the village of Achnasheen in Wester Ross. The hotel features a variety of different room, from single occupancy to a suite with a four-poster bed, with all rooms complete with an en-suite, a TV and tea and coffee making facilities. A full Scottish breakfast is served the following morning.

The onsite restaurant serves fresh and locally sourced seasonal produce as well as a variety of drinks including local Scottish whiskies.

///inched.bounding.slimy

MIDGE BITE CAFE, Achnasheen

The Midge Bite Cafe is a friendly coffee shop located in Achnasheen in the heart of the Scottish Highlands. The staff are open to adapting options on the menu to suit your dietary requirements, however their are a lot of options of the menu for those with vegetarian and vegan dietary requirements. A great place to stop off between Torridon and Inverness.

///sniff.stormy.dollar

KINLOCHEWE CARAVAN AND MOTORHOME CLUB CAMPSITE, Kinlochewe

Kinlochewe Campsite is an unforgettable place to stay in the Wester Ross region. Located at the foot of the towering Beinn Eighe, this campsite has a slow and peaceful feel to it. The small village of Kinlochewe is only a short walk away, where you will find a shop, a petrol station, a cafe and a hotel. Kinlochewe campsite is located at the end of the drive along Glen Docherty from Achnasheen and this is a drive that will never tire. The spectacular views of the surrounding mountains towering above you and the high chances of you seeing deer roaming around in the fields around you, make this part of the world very special. Kinlochewe is a perfect base for keen walkers and hikers due to the close proximity of the mountains. The Scottish Natural Heritage Beinn Eighe and Loch Maree Islands National Nature Reserve is nearby where you will have the opportunity to spot golden eagles or deer by the Loch.
///pitching.huts.chains

KINLOCHEWE HOTEL, Kinlochewe

Kinlochewe Hotel is a building with a lot of history, dating back to the 1800s when it was built. Hugh Munro – who 'munros' were named after– stayed in the hotel during 1899 and 1900. This is a perfect base location for those travelling the NC500 as there are plenty of things to do nearby, including many walks the sights and nature of Loch Maree.

Kinlochewe Hotel has a variety of rooms that include single rooms, twin rooms and double rooms. The rooms have en-suite or private bathrooms and two of the rooms share a bathroom, perfect for a family to share. A full Scottish breakfast is served the following morning after your arrival.

The restaurant at Kinlochewe Hotel strives to serve delicious home-cooked meals using locally sourced products. It can also cater for those with special dietary requirements: if you mention to the staff they will be able to assist you.
///embedded.skinning.sprinting

A highland cow takes in the view, Torridon

TORRIDON STORES AND CAFE, Torridon

Sitting at the tip of Upper Loch Torridon are the small and cosy cafe and stores of the village of Torridon. Here at Torridon Stores and Cafe, you can enjoy a hot drink and a freshly baked cake, or something more filling, such as the homemade soup, toasted sandwiches, or hot filled-rolls. The cafe area has a warm and friendly atmosphere, with log-burners to add to the ambience.
///grudging.named.aced

TORRIDON YOUTH HOSTEL, Torridon

Torridon Youth Hostel is conveniently located at the head of Upper Loch Torridon and is a great base for outdoor enthusiasts exploring the area. Liathach, an impressive mountain with two peaks of munro status and an extremely challenging ridge walk, towers over the hostel.

The Torridon Youth Hostel features a well-equipped kitchen, or you also have the option to opt for a continental breakfast during your stay. There is a large drying room for your kit and basic provisions are available to purchase at reception with the closest shop being around a 15 minute walk away.
///happen.variances.horizons

WEE WHISTLE STOP CAFE, Torridon

With beautiful floor-to-ceiling views from the windows of the Wee Whistle Stop Cafe, you will struggle to find a better spot to enjoy a fresh coffee and homemade cake. The Loch Torridon Community Hall opened the cafe in 2019, which offers an ever-changing menu of local and seasonal produce for guests to enjoy in a comfortable environment.

Open from early during the week, the Wee Whistle Stop is a great place to stop-off for a bite to eat before a big day out, or to pop in for a large and nutritious lunch after a busy day spent in the highlands.
///online.ground.brimmed

STAY
£££

EAT
£££

STAY
£

THE BOATHOUSE, Annat

This secluded self-catering accommodation sits on the banks of Upper Loch Torridon near Annat and is a fantastic place to stay if you are looking to escape the hustle and bustle of life and find some tranquillity. The Boathouse has exclusive views out to Upper Loch Torridon where you can look out for wildlife while exploring the surrounding area. The interior in the Boathouse is very stylish with a contemporary feel; there are two bedrooms, a kitchen and beautiful living area with a wood-burner keeping the space cosy, making it a true home away from home experience.
///waltzed.twists.bulbs

BO & MUC, Annat

The Bo & Muc restaurant is located in the Torridon resort and is a great place to go for a bite to eat or a drink after a day on the hills. Seasonal and locally sourced produce is served at Bo & Muc, using a field-to-fork approach and there is a two-acre garden where the fruit and vegetables are grown. There is a small selection of dishes on the menu, each one crafted with amazing attention to detail in how it looks and tastes.
///awesome.officers.remembers

FERROCH HOUSE, Annat

Ferroch House is a cosy guesthouse located in Annat with spectacular views across Loch Torridon. There are two parts to the guest house, which can be rented individually or together. This self-catering accommodation feels like a home away from home with cosy and comfortable bedrooms, a fully equipped kitchen with laundry facilities and a cosy fireplace in the living room.

Ferroch House is a great base for those wanting to explore the Torridon area.
///frizz.broadcast.prongs

Shieldaig Lodge, Shieldaig

THE TORRIDON, Annat

The Torridon Hotel is a very luxurious 5-star place to stay in Wester Ross. There are 18 unique bedrooms decorated beautifully with a touch of combined Scottish and Victorian heritage. All of the bedrooms are very spacious and come in a variety of sizes from classic to the Torridon Master Suite.

The Torridon Hotel has a restaurant for residents and the Beinn Bar is open for tea, coffee and cake throughout the day for both residents and non-residents.
///absorb.thanks.glad

SHIELDAIG CAMPING AND CABINS, Shieldaig

Shieldaig Camping and Cabins is the ideal place to stay in Wester Ross with panoramic views across to Shieldaig Island. This elevated location overlooks the small fishing village of Shieldaig, and is within a short walking distance to shops and restaurants along the bay. Shieldaig Camping and Cabins is a family run business that opened in 2019 and has since been extremely popular with those visiting the Wester Ross area or touring the North Coast 500 route. The campsite has 20 powered hard-standing pitches for motorhomes or caravans, as well as a number of pitches for small tents.

The luxury cabins have a private decking area with prime views across the bay where you might be lucky enough to see a pod of dolphins swimming or the most stunning sunset.
///thatched.probe.sketches

SHIELDAIG LODGE, Shieldaig

EAT & STAY £££

The Shieldaig Lodge is a beautiful hotel set in a 26,000 acre estate that has views across the loch, the village of Shieldaig and Shieldaig Bay from the lodge and large garden area. Dating back to the 19th century, this was originally an old hunting lodge, which was later used as a hospital during the Second World War.

There are a number of en-suite bedrooms, four of which are dog friendly, and all rooms have delightful views over the hills or Loch Shieldaig. In the morning you can expect a full Scottish breakfast. The Shieldaig Lodge features cosy lounges where you can enjoy a whisky by a cosy fire after a day of exploring.

In the restaurant, you can expect a delicious meal, made from fresh locally sourced produce and led by Head Chef, Jerome Prodanu. The walled garden has recently been renovated to reinstate a vegetable garden, allowing fresh produce to grow right outside the hotel.

Gairloch is a 10 minute drive from the Shieldaig Lodge and Badachro is a short drive in the other direction. Make sure to look out to the loch during your stay and you may see some seals swimming around.
///glows.gravitate.bribing

APPLECROSS CAMPSITE, Applecross

STAY £

The Applecross Campsite sits above the small village of Applecross on the peninsula, north-west of Kyle of Lochalsh. Featuring over six acres of camping space and fantastic views across to the Black Cuillin on the Isle of Skye, as well as the islands of Raasay and Rona, The Applecross Campsite has become a popular place to stay on Scotland's west coast.

Six-berth rental caravans and camping huts are also available to rent for overnight stays at the Applecross Campsite.
///blazers.stuck.formless

The view from the top of the Bealach Na Ba, the famous road leading to Applecross

APPLECROSS INN, Applecross

The Applecross Inn is a very popular place to visit on the Applecross peninsula, serving up delicious food with outstanding views. On a warm sunny day in Scotland, this is a great place to be. There are seven sea view en-suite bedrooms available on a bed-and-breakfast basis and Judith and her staff will ensure you have a comfortable and welcoming stay.
///rash.rewarded.severe

EAT &
STAY
££

APPLECROSS INN-SIDE-OUT, Applecross

Applecross Inn-Side-Out is a food trailer serving delicious hot food and cakes outside the Applecross Inn on the seafront. The Applecross Inn is often booked out, so this allows for visitors or locals to order take-aways from the basic menu. The fish and chips are a popular choice and the handmade ice-cream is delightful by the sea on a warm sunny day.
///vocally.scrapping.download

EAT
££

KISHORN SEAFOOD BAR, Ardarroch

For those that love seafood, the Kishorn Seafood Bar is a real treat to visit when you are in the area. Overlooking Skye and the Applecross peninsula, the Kishorn Seafood Bar aims to serve the best locally sourced seafood that is full of flavour.

The Kishorn Seafood Bar was established in 1996. However, it has recently come into the hands of new owners who are committed to supporting sustainability and local suppliers. The catch is delivered daily and includes hand-dived scallops, lobsters and langoustines. A must visit for a seafood lover.
///fidgeted.scoots.promise

EAT
£££

NC5OO

SANACHAN BUNKHOUSE, Ardarroch

Sanachan Bunkhouse is a great place to stay if you are looking for somewhere comfortable and affordable with easy access to the hills. The bedroom is shared with other guests and can sleep up to 15 guests between two dorms. There are great shared facilities in the home for you to come back to after a busy day exploring such as a hot power shower, a drying room for your

STAY
£

kit, a kitchen and a comfortable seating area with a log burner. Sanachan Bunkhouse is a self-catering accommodation with a fully equipped kitchen and a fridge and freezer.
///cans.residual.investors

EAT
£

ALBATROSS CAFE, Lochcarron

With stunning views over the still waters of Lochcarron, the Albatross cafe is a fantastic spot to enjoy some homemade food from a small, family run cafe. Situated at the Lochcarron Golf Club, the Albatross cafe is a popular food spot for those relaxing after a game of golf and for visitors passing through the highlands.

Open from morning till late afternoon during the week, the Albatross provides both breakfast and lunch options to guests. Hot filled rolls, homemade soup with fresh bread, and delicious sandwiches make up the simple and wholesome menu in this small cafe.
///pushover.examiner.plan

EAT
££

THE BISTRO LOCHCARRON, Lochcarron

In the heart of the small highland village of Lochcarron, the Bistro is a unique dining experience featuring a one-man, open kitchen serving up local and seasonally sourced ingredients. The head chef, Sean, takes great pride in the dishes he produces, preparing everything in-house including the butchery and bakery for all of the dishes that are served at the Bistro. By mixing classic French and Italian dishes with the freshest Scottish produce, the Bistro delivers a mouthwatering array that never fails to encourage customers back for more.
///bloom.flirts.weeknight

EAT &
STAY
£

ROCKVILLA GUEST HOUSE, Lochcarron

Rockvilla Guest House is situated in the picturesque village of Lochcarron with beautiful views across the loch. This small, family run business will welcome you to their comfortable guest house and ensure you have an enjoyable and comfortable stay.

Applecross Walled Garden (top) and Applecross Bay (bottom), Applecross

There are three recently renovated modern and spacious rooms at Rockvilla Guest House, two with en-suite and one with a private bathroom. All rooms have exceptional loch views where you may be lucky enough to see some dolphins or otters. There is also a self-contained apartment sleeping two to three people at the rear of the building, however this does not have loch views.

Rockvilla has a licensed restaurant and bar with a great locally sourced selection of food on the menu and stunning views to match from the outdoor seating area.
///disprove.irrigate.intend

THE WEE CAMPSITE, Lochcarron
Nestled in the heart of Wester Ross and surrounded by the most beautiful mountainous scenery, sits The Wee Campsite. With incredible views of Loch Carron and the Attadale Hills, it is a very popular place to pitch a tent or take a caravan or motorhome on the NC500. This campsite is over 70 years old and has been adapted over the years and has an elevated location overlooking the loch. It is within a short walking distance to the shops and restaurants in the village that can be accessed by a path.
///earth.nourished.clashing

APPLECROSS WALLED GARDEN, Strathcarron
Sitting on the outskirts of the main street in Applecross is the Walled Garden, a picturesque Victorian Walled Garden and cafe area with indoor and outdoor seating. It is believed that the garden has been around since 1675 when Applecross House was built. Having become derelict between the wars and in the 1950s, it was finally revived in 2001, when Jon and Elaine created a tearoom in the abandoned walled garden. They wholeheartedly believe that sustainability is a way of life, not only in what we eat, but also in supporting young people in this remote part of Scotland.

All fruits and vegetables are grown in the organic gardens, seafood is caught locally in the bay and meats are croft-raised. The award-winning scones are a must-try with hot chocolate on your visit to the Applecross Walled Garden.
///zipped.stunts.relishing

THE BOTHY, Strathcarron

EAT
££

The Bothy is one of the more unique accommodations on the NC500, similar to a traditional Scottish bothy with a little more comfort. This accommodation is completely off grid, no heating, no electricity but magical views. The Bothy is located within the Ben Damph Estate, looking over Upper Loch Torridon and surrounded by nature.

The Bothy has an outer area and two inner areas. In the outer area is a dining table and a basic kitchen area with a canister of drinking water and a gas cooker. In both of the inner rooms there are two single beds that can be pushed together and a fireplace with wood and kindling. Guests can either bring their own sleeping bags or alternatively can add a bed package as an additional extra upon booking. Outside, there is a composting toilet and separate shower area.

As the sun sets in the evening, you will see the most beautiful golden glow through the extensive glass windows and you may even see deer roaming around in the grass in front of The Bothy.
///totally.charge.barbarian

CARRON RESTAURANT, Strathcarron

EAT
££

NC500

If you are looking for a great place to eat in Strathcarron, Carron Restaurant has a great menu of light bites and main meals that can be enjoyed in its indoor or outdoor seating area. The home-cooked food served at the Carron Restaurant is seasonal and sourced locally and can be enjoyed with a glass of wine from the wide selection on offer. There is a wide range of whisky sold in their shop as well.
///crunching.evoked.released

View of Loch Carron from the village of Lochcarron

SHIELDAIG BAR AND KITCHEN, Strathcarron

EAT
££

With a beautiful view overlooking Loch Shieldaig, the Shieldaig Bar and Kitchen, a former hunting lodge, is a great place to enjoy a meal on the NC500. There is a thriving atmosphere inside with views looking across the Loch. Alternatively, you can sit outside and soak up the views.

They have an extensive menu at the Shieldaig Bar and Kitchen, which caters to all dietary requirements. If you enjoy a wood-fired pizza, upstairs there is an open pizza oven where you can watch your dinner being made from scratch.
///brink.ferrets.flaking

STRATHCARRON STATION HOUSE, Strathcarron

STAY
£

NC5⊙O

A luxurious stay in a restored building from 1870, right on the station platform in Strathcarron. This two-bedroom first-floor apartment is perfect for those who enjoy watching one of the eight trains a day go by on the Kyle Line, a world-famous line and one of the "Great Railway Journeys". Strathcarron Station house has two double bedrooms, a self-catering kitchen area and free laundry facilities.

There are two accommodations available to book at Strathcarron Station House. The bottom floor is fully accessible, however the top floor accommodation is not.
///playroom.intricate.simply

INDEX

Note: page numbers in **bold** refer to information contained in captions.

PHOTO CREDITS